CONTEMPORARY'S
LOOK AT THE U·S·
BOOK 1

CAROLE CROSS
ESL Coordinator
El Monte–Rosemead Adult School
El Monte, California

with

ROB PARAL
Research Associate
NALEO (National Association of
Latino Elected and Appointed Officials)
Washington, D.C.

Project Coordinator
Julie Landau

Editor
Betsy Rubin

CB
CONTEMPORARY
BOOKS
CHICAGO · NEW YORK

Library of Congress Cataloging-in-Publication Data

Cross, Carole.
   Look at the U.S.
(An ESL/civics series)
Cover title: Contemporary's look at the U.S.
"Based on the federal citizenship texts."
   1. Civics.   I. Title.   II. Title: Look at the US.
III. Title: Contemporary's look at the U.S.   IV. Series.
JK1758.C76   1989   320.473   88-34092
ISBN 0-8092-4387-3

Photo credits
Page 1: The Bettmann Archive. Page 3: H. S. Rice. Courtesy, Department of Library Services, American Museum of Natural History (Negative 312686). Pages 7 and 11: The Bettmann Archive. Pages 15 and 17: Culver Pictures. Pages 19, 23, and 25: The Bettmann Archive. Page 29: Culver Pictures. Pages 37 and 41: The Bettmann Archive. Page 45: Culver Pictures. Page 49: The Bettmann Archive. Page 51: AP/Wide World Photos. Page 55: UPI/Bettmann Newsphotos. Page 57: © George Bellerose/Stock Boston. Page 59: © Daniel S. Brody/Stock Boston. Page 65: UPI/Bettmann Newsphotos. Page 69: © Owen Franken/Stock Boston. Pages 71, 73, and 77: AP/Wide World Photos. Page 79: UPI/Bettmann Newsphotos. Page 83: AP/Wide World Photos. Page 87: Culver Pictures. Page 91: © Burt Glinn/Magnum Photos.

Published by Contemporary Books, Inc.
180 North Michigan Avenue, Chicago, Illinois 60601
Manufactured in the United States of America
International Standard Book Number: 0-8092-4387-3

Published simultaneously in Canada by
Beaverbooks, Ltd.
195 Allstate Parkway
Valleywood Business Park
Markham, Ontario L3R 4T8
Canada

Editorial Director Caren Van Slyke	*Cover Design* Lois Koehler
Editorial Kathy Osmus Craig Bolt Lisa Dillman Susan Grzyb	*Illustrator* Rosemary Morrissey-Herzberg *Photo Researcher* Julie Laffin
Editorial/Production Manager Patricia Reid	*Art & Production* Princess Louise El
Production Editor Craig Bolt	*Typography* Carol Schoder

Cover photo © Index Stock International, Inc.

Contents

To the Instructor

The *Look at the U.S.* series was specially designed to help ESL teachers introduce civics concepts into the classroom. This multi-level series introduces the fundamentals of U.S. history and government and is based on the federal citizenship textbooks. This flexible series can serve as texts for:

- special ESL/civics classes for amnesty students
- citizenship classes
- standard ESL classes

In addition to this book, *Look at the U.S., Book 1*, the series includes:

- *Look at the U.S., Book 2*
- *Teacher's Guide, Books 1 & 2*
- *Look at the U.S., Literacy Level*
- *Teacher's Guide, Literacy Level*

Instructional Design for This Book

The purpose of this book is to teach the basics of U.S. history and government by reinforcing the English language skills of listening, speaking, reading, and writing. To accomplish this, each lesson incorporates the features shown on the chart below.

Books 1 & 2—Lesson Design

FEATURE *(per lesson)*	SKILL	SOURCE
Setting the Stage	listening and speaking	teacher's guide
Before You Read	listening, speaking, and pre-reading	student text
Reading Passage	reading	student text
After You Read	reading comprehension	student text
Think About . . .	speaking, listening, or writing	student text
Using New Words	vocabulary development	student text
Sentence Completion (*Book 1*)	writing	student text
Express Your Ideas (*Book 2*)	writing	student text
These optional activities can be presented at the teacher's discretion:		
Listening Activity	listening and speaking	teacher's guide
Group Activity	listening and speaking	teacher's guide
Writing Activity	writing	teacher's guide

Activities found in the teacher's guide should be used to supplement the text and, most importantly, to actively draw the students into the learning process.

Teacher's Guide for Books 1 and 2

The teacher's guide for Books 1 and 2 provides:

- an overview of the key components of each lesson
- chapter-by-chapter ideas for supplementary classroom activities
- handouts to use in the classroom

Throughout your work with this series, you will be given the opportunity to link important issues in American government and history to concerns facing your students in their daily lives. In particular, teacher's guide activities will help you relate civics topics to everyday life.

The Multi-Level Approach

Books 1 and 2 address the same key concepts in U.S. history and government. However, since students have varying degrees of proficiency in English, the books are written at different levels. Book 1 is aimed at students who can speak, read, and write some basic English and who have had some education in their own country. Book 2 assumes a higher educational level and greater fluency in English.

Book 1 may be too difficult for some of the beginning-level students. For this reason, there is a literacy-level book (and accompanying teacher's guide) in the *Look at the U.S.* series.

For more information on other books in this series, contact:

Contemporary Books
Adult Education Division
180 North Michigan Avenue
Chicago, Ilinois 60601

Our toll-free number is 1-800-621-1918.

For more information on how to use this book and for additional classroom activities, see *Look at the U.S. Teacher's Guide—Books 1 & 2.*

U.S. History

New arrivals to the U.S. in the 1800s.

Chapter 1
Native Americans

Many Native Americans lived in villages.

BEFORE YOU READ

1. The people in the picture are Native Americans. What does "native" mean?

2. What is your native country?

3. How do you think Native Americans traveled?

4. How do you think Native Americans got their food?

5. The picture shows a Native American village. What is a village?

Native Americans

Thousands of years ago, the two continents of Asia and North America were not separate. They were connected by a small piece of land. People lived in Asia, but there were no people in North and South America.

Then people came to North America from Asia. They walked across the small piece of land connecting the two continents. These people came because they were looking for food. They were hunters—people who followed and killed animals to eat.

Over many years, more people came from Asia to North and South America. They settled there and made that land their home. Today, we call these people Native Americans, or Indians.

In some places, the Native Americans found wild plants such as berries and nuts to eat. Then some groups learned to grow their own plants. They did not have to travel to find food anymore, so they could stay in one place. As a result, some groups formed villages. In these villages, they learned to raise animals such as turkeys. They also grew many new plants such as corn, tomatoes, and tobacco.

Later, people from Europe came to North America. The Europeans learned many things from the Native Americans. For example, they learned how to grow corn and other food. However, these new people tried to control the Native Americans. Often, they took the land away from them.

Today, Native Americans still live in North and South America. Native Americans have played an important part in the history and culture of the United States.

WORDS TO KNOW	PLACES TO KNOW
continent	Asia
hunter	North America
settle	South America
village	Europe
raise	

AFTER YOU READ

Circle True (T) or False (F).

T   F   1. People have always lived in North America.

T   F   2. People walked from North America to Asia.

T   F   3. Some Native Americans formed villages.

T   F   4. Europeans sometimes took land from the Native Americans.

T   F   5. Today there are no Native Americans in the U.S.

THINK ABOUT NATIVE AMERICANS

Answer the following questions.

1. Why did the first people come to North America?

2. How did they come here?

3. In the beginning, how did the Native Americans get their food?

4. Later, villages were formed. How did people get their food then?

5. Where do many Native Americans live today?

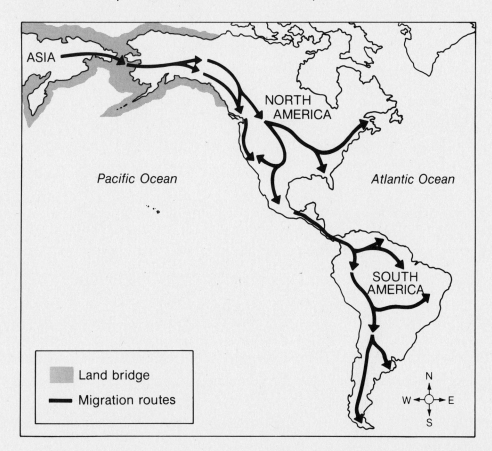

Thousands of years ago, people crossed a small piece of land to come from Asia to North America.

USING NEW WORDS

Complete the following sentences by using the words below.

settled   raised   continents   Indians   hunted

1. Asia, North America, and South America are all _____.

2. At first, Native Americans _____ animals for food. They followed and killed them.

3. Different groups of people _____ in North and South America and made that land their home.

4. In their villages, Native Americans _____ animals and plants for food.

5. Native Americans are also called _____.

SENTENCE COMPLETION

Think about what you have read and complete the sentences below.

1. People came to North America from Asia because _____
   _____.

2. Hunters were people who _____
   _____.

3. Some groups did not have to travel for food, so _____
   _____.

4. Native Americans grew new plants such as _____
   _____.

Answers for this chapter start on page 108.

Chapter 2
Christopher Columbus and the New World

Christopher Columbus claimed the New World for the Queen of Spain.

BEFORE YOU READ

1. Why did you come to the United States?

2. Why do people travel to new countries?

3. How did Columbus travel to the New World?

4. In what other ways did people travel at the time of Columbus?

5. What do you think Columbus was looking for when he crossed the ocean?

Christopher Columbus

At the time of Columbus, people traveled from Europe to Asia to buy goods like silk and spices. These things were very valuable, so Europeans would travel great distances to get them. People went from Europe to Asia by land, and the trip was long and difficult.

Christopher Columbus thought there was another way to get to Asia. He believed that the earth was round, like a ball. For this reason, he thought that he could cross the Atlantic Ocean to get to Asia. He asked the Queen of Spain for help. She gave him three ships: the *Nina*, the *Pinta*, and the *Santa Maria*. She also gave Columbus men to sail in the ships with him.

Many people thought that Columbus was crazy. They thought the earth was flat, and they said that his ships would fall off the end of the earth. They were wrong, of course, and Columbus sailed across the Atlantic Ocean in the year 1492.

When Columbus reached land, he thought that he was in India, on the continent of Asia. For this reason, he called the people that he saw "Indians." Later, people realized that Columbus had come to a completely new land, and they called this land the New World. Today the New World is called North America and South America.

WORDS TO KNOW	PEOPLE TO KNOW	PLACES TO KNOW
goods	Columbus	Europe
travel	Queen of Spain	Asia
trip		India
sail		
ship		

AFTER YOU READ

Circle True (T) or False (F).

T   F   **1.** Columbus wanted to find the New World.

T   F   **2.** Columbus wanted to travel to Asia by land.

T   F   **3.** Columbus first came to the New World in 1492.

T   F   **4.** The Queen of England helped Columbus.

T   F   **5.** Columbus sailed to the New World with three ships.

THINK ABOUT COLUMBUS

Answer the following questions.

1. At the time of Columbus, how did people travel from Europe to Asia?

2. Why did Columbus sail across the ocean?

3. Why do you think that Columbus asked the Queen of Spain for help?

4. When Columbus came to the New World, why did he think he was in India?

5. How did Columbus change history?

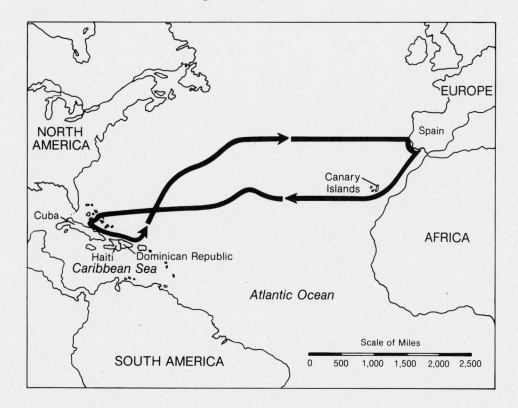

This map shows how Columbus traveled to the New World and back to Spain.

USING NEW WORDS

Complete the following sentences by using the words below.

ships   New World   goods   valuable   round

1. In Asia, people could buy valuable _____.

2. Columbus thought the earth was _____.

3. Columbus and his men crossed the ocean in three _____.

4. Silk and spices were very _____.

5. Instead of reaching India, Columbus came to the _____.

SENTENCE COMPLETION

Think about what you have read and complete the sentences below.

1. Europeans went to Asia because _____

_____.

2. Europeans traveled to Asia by land, but Columbus _____

_____.

3. To help Columbus, the Queen of Spain _____

_____.

4. In 1492, Columbus tried to reach Asia, but _____

_____.

Answers for this chapter start on page 108.

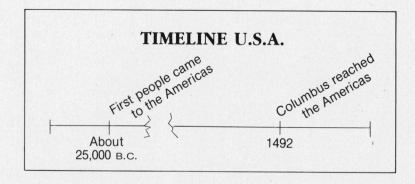

10

Chapter 3
Jamestown and Plymouth

Native Americans and settlers eating the first Thanksgiving dinner.

BEFORE YOU READ

1. What was your first year in the United States like?

2. Is it hard to start a new life in a new land? Why?

3. What is a colony? Do you know who formed the first colonies in North America?

4. Why do you think people came to settle in the New World?

5. Do you think life was easy or hard in the colonies? Why?

11

Jamestown and Plymouth

Many years after Columbus, more Europeans came to live in North America. Many of these people came from England. They started colonies, or communities, in the eastern part of North America.

The first permanent English settlement was Jamestown. In 1607, 105 English people formed this colony. It was in the southeastern part of North America, now the state of Virginia.

In 1620, another group of English people formed the colony of Plymouth. Plymouth was north of Jamestown in an area that is now the state of Massachusetts. The settlers came to this place on a ship called the *Mayflower.*

The settlers of Plymouth were called the Pilgrims. The Pilgrims came to North America for religious reasons. They had no religious freedom in England. The Pilgrims thought they would be free to have their own religion in North America.

At first, life was difficult at Plymouth. The Pilgrims were sick and hungry, and many died. However, they worked hard and planted food. The Native Americans also helped them and gave them food. Finally, the Pilgrims had enough to eat. In the autumn of 1621, they had a big celebration. They wanted to give thanks for all of their food.

Today, Americans call this celebration Thanksgiving Day. It is celebrated on the fourth Thursday in November. On Thanksgiving, families come together to eat the traditional food of the Pilgrims and the Indians. On that day, people also give thanks for their health and their families.

WORDS TO KNOW	PEOPLE TO KNOW	PLACES TO KNOW
settlement the *Mayflower* religion Thanksgiving Day	Pilgrims	England Jamestown Plymouth

AFTER YOU READ

Circle True (T) or False (F).

T   F   **1.** Jamestown was the first permanent English settlement.

T   F   **2.** Jamestown and Plymouth were in the western part of North America.

T   F   **3.** The Pilgrims came in a ship called the *Santa Maria*.

T   F   **4.** The Pilgrims had no religious freedom in England.

T   F   **5.** Life was easy for the Pilgrims during their first year at Plymouth.

THINK ABOUT JAMESTOWN AND PLYMOUTH

Answer the following questions.

1. When did English people form the colony of Jamestown?

2. Why did the Pilgrims come to North America?

3. What problems did the Pilgrims have in their first year at Plymouth?

4. Why did the Pilgrims have a great celebration?

5. Why is Thanksgiving Day an important holiday in the U.S.?

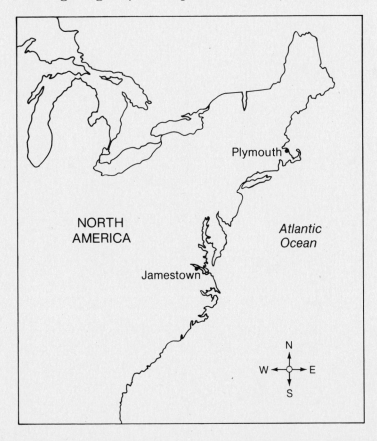

This map of the eastern United States shows Jamestown and Plymouth.

13

USING NEW WORDS

Complete the following sentences by using the words below.

Plymouth   Jamestown   colonies   religious   Thanksgiving

1. People left Europe to form _____ in North America.

2. The first English settlement in North America was _____.

3. The Pilgrims created a colony at _____.

4. The Pilgrims had no _____ freedom in England.

5. The Pilgrims celebrated the first _____.

SENTENCE COMPLETION

Think about what you have read and complete the sentences below.

1. Jamestown was the first _____.

2. In 1607 people came to Jamestown, and in 1620 _____

   _____.

3. At first, life was difficult for the Pilgrims because _____

   _____.

4. Today, Thanksgiving is celebrated on _____.

Answers for this chapter start on page 108.

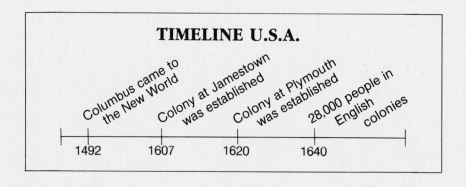

TIMELINE U.S.A.

Columbus came to the New World — 1492

Colony at Jamestown was established — 1607

Colony at Plymouth was established — 1620

28,000 people in English colonies — 1640

Chapter 4
Beginnings of the Revolution

Angry colonists threw tea into Boston Harbor to protest a tax on tea.

BEFORE YOU READ

1. What are the people in the picture doing?

2. What is a tax? Do you like to pay taxes?

3. What is a colony?

4. Why do some countries have colonies?

5. Why did the American colonists want to be independent from England?

Rebellion in the Colonies

In the 1700s, England formed many colonies in the eastern part of North America. The English government controlled these colonies in many ways.

The colonies were not permitted to trade with other countries. In other words, they sent goods only to England and bought goods only from England. Also, the people of the colonies, called colonists, had to pay high taxes to England. Finally, English soldiers were in the colonies. All in all, the colonists were not happy, and they decided to protest.

In 1770, a group of colonists began to protest in Boston, Massachusetts. They went to an English government building, and they started to yell at the English soldiers there. The soldiers became nervous and fired their guns at the protesters. The protesters did not have guns. In all, the soldiers killed five colonists. This was called the Boston Massacre. It was the beginning of the rebellion by the colonists.

Several years later, in 1773, another group of colonists in Boston got together to protest. The English government had put a tax on tea, and the colonists did not want to pay it.

The colonists planned a special protest against this tax. About 60 colonists dressed up as Indians. Then they went on an English ship full of tea in Boston Harbor. The colonists threw the tea into the ocean to protest the tax on tea. This became known as the Boston Tea Party, and it made the English angry.

The Boston Massacre and the Boston Tea Party started a spirit of rebellion among the colonists. People from the different colonies began to work together against the English government.

WORDS TO KNOW	EVENTS TO KNOW	PLACES TO KNOW
colonists	Boston Massacre	North America
taxes	Boston Tea Party	Boston
soldiers		Boston Harbor

AFTER YOU READ

Circle True (T) or False (F).

T   F   1. The colonists paid taxes to England.

T   F   2. The colonists were happy to pay taxes to England.

T   F   3. The colonists protested against English taxes.

T   F   4. At the Boston Tea Party, colonists dressed like Indians and threw tea into the harbor.

T   F   5. During the Boston Tea Party, English soldiers killed five colonists.

THINK ABOUT REBELLION IN THE COLONIES

Answer the following questions.

1. Why were the colonists unhappy with England?

2. How did the Boston Massacre begin?

3. How many colonists died in the Boston Massacre?

4. During the Boston Tea Party, why did the colonists throw tea into the harbor?

5. How do you think the colonists felt after the Boston Massacre and the Boston Tea Party?

In the Boston Massacre, English soldiers shot and killed American colonists.

USING NEW WORDS

Complete the following sentences by using the words below.

tax   guns   rebellion   protested   colonists

1. England put a _____ on tea.

2. The _____ did not want to pay the tax to England.

3. The colonists _____ against the tax.

4. The soldiers fired their _____ at the colonists.

5. The Boston Tea Party was an act of _____.

SENTENCE COMPLETION

Think about what you have read and complete the sentences below.

1. The colonists were angry with England because _____

_____.

2. A group of colonists went to a government building and _____

_____.

3. During the Boston Massacre, the English soldiers _____

_____.

4. During the Boston Tea Party, some colonists _____

_____.

Answers for this chapter start on page 109.

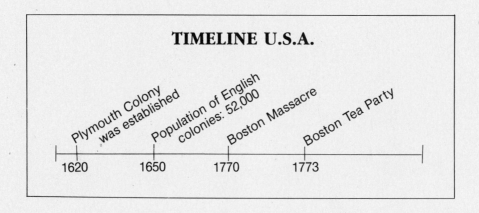

TIMELINE U.S.A.

Plymouth Colony was established — Population of English colonies: 52,000 — Boston Massacre — Boston Tea Party

1620   1650   1770   1773

Chapter 5
The Declaration of Independence

A representative signs the Declaration of Independence.

BEFORE YOU READ

1. What makes a person independent?

2. What makes a country independent?

3. Why did the colonists want to be independent from England?

4. On what date does the U.S. celebrate its independence?

5. Does your native country have a national holiday? What does it celebrate?

The Declaration of Independence

In 1776, there were 13 colonies in North America. All of the colonies wanted independence from England. Representatives of the colonies decided to write a document to declare their independence. This document is called the Declaration of Independence.

Thomas Jefferson was a representative of Virginia, and he wrote most of the Declaration of Independence. Later, Thomas Jefferson became the third president of the United States.

The Declaration says many things. It says that the colonies decided to be "Free and Independent States." It explains why the colonies did not want to be under the control of the King of England.

The Declaration also states that "all men are created equal." It says that a government cannot take away the people's basic rights. These are the rights to "life, liberty, and the pursuit of happiness."

The representatives of the 13 colonies met in Philadelphia, Pennsylvania, on July 4, 1776. On that day, they approved the Declaration of Independence. That day was the beginning of the United States as an independent nation. Today, we celebrate Independence Day, or the Fourth of July, as the nation's birthday.

WORDS TO KNOW	PEOPLE TO KNOW	PLACES TO KNOW
representatives independence Declaration of Independence rights Independence Day	Thomas Jefferson King of England	Philadelphia Pennsylvania

AFTER YOU READ

Circle True (T) or False (F).

T   F   1. There were 20 colonies in 1776.

T   F   2. On July 4, the Declaration of Independence was signed.

T   F   3. The colonists wanted to have their own government.

T   F   4. Thomas Jefferson wrote most of the Declaration of Independence.

T   F   5. The Fourth of July is a national holiday in England.

THINK ABOUT THE DECLARATION OF INDEPENDENCE

Answer the following questions.

1. How many colonies were there in 1776?
2. Why did the colonists write the Declaration of Independence?
3. What happened on July 4, 1776?
4. What does the Declaration of Independence talk about?
5. How do you think that the King of England felt about the Declaration of Independence?

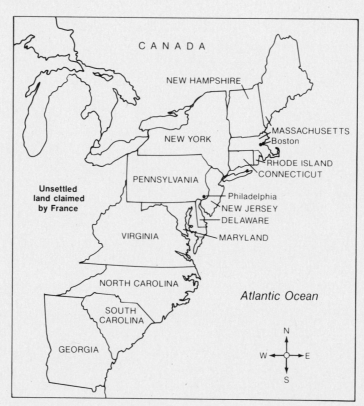

These 13 colonies declared their independence from England in 1776.

USING NEW WORDS

Complete the following sentences by using the words below.

representatives   Independence Day
rights   approved   independent

1. Life and liberty are two basic _____.

2. In July 1776, a group of men _____ the Declaration of
Independence.

3. The _____ of the colonies signed the Declaration of
Independence.

4. The Fourth of July is also called _____.

5. The colonies wanted to be _____ from England.

SENTENCE COMPLETION

Think about what you have read and complete the sentences below.

1. On July 4, 1776, representatives of the colonies _____

_____.

2. The Declaration of Independence says that _____

_____.

3. The Declaration of Independence was written because _____

_____.

4. July 4 is called the nation's birthday because _____

_____.

Answers for this chapter start on page 109.

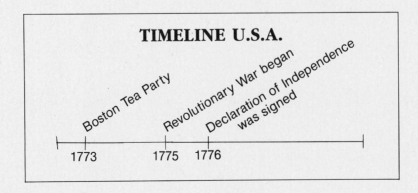

Chapter 6
George Washington and the Revolution

George Washington and his men fought many battles.

BEFORE YOU READ

1. What is a revolutionary war?

2. What can cause a revolutionary war?

3. Has your native country ever had a revolutionary war?

4. Who were some important early leaders of your native country?

5. Why was George Washington famous?

Revolution and the Nation's First Leader

George Washington is one of the most famous Americans in history. He was born in Virginia on February 22, 1732. By the time he died, he was known as "The Father of His Country." George Washington was the first president of the United States. Before that, he was the leader of the American Revolutionary War against the English. He was the commander of the colonial army in this war.

As you know, the colonists first began to organize together after the Boston Massacre and the Boston Tea Party. Then, in April of 1775, the Revolutionary War began. It started in the colony of Massachusetts.

In Lexington, Massachusetts, a colonist named Paul Revere and his companions rode through the streets on horses. They told the people that the British (English) were coming. As a result, the colonists were prepared for the invasion.

When the English marched into Lexington, the colonists surprised them with their guns. Eight colonists died in the fight at Lexington, but only one English soldier was hurt.

Then the English soldiers left Lexington and went to the town of Concord, Massachusetts. At Concord, about 350 colonists attacked the English. The English left Concord to go to Boston, but thousands of colonists attacked them on the way. This was the start of the Revolutionary War.

George Washington was the leader of many battles, or fights, in this war. In October of 1781, Washington's army fought against thousands of English soldiers at Yorktown, Virginia. Washington's army won this important battle. This battle showed the English that the colonists were strong. Two years later, in 1783, the war ended. The colonists won, and the United States became an independent country.

WORDS TO KNOW	PEOPLE TO KNOW	PLACES TO KNOW
commander army invasion	George Washington Paul Revere	Massachusetts Lexington Concord Yorktown

AFTER YOU READ

Circle True (T) or False (F).

T   F   1. George Washington was known as "The Father of His Country."

T   F   2. Washington was the third president of the United States.

T   F   3. The first battles of the Revolutionary War were at Lexington and Concord.

T   F   4. Washington's army lost the battle at Yorktown.

T   F   5. The colonists won the Revolutionary War in 1783.

THINK ABOUT THE AMERICAN REVOLUTION

Answer the following questions.

1. In what year did the Revolutionary War begin?
2. When did the war end?
3. Who won the Revolutionary War?
4. Why did the colonists want independence?
5. England was a strong country, but the colonists won the war. How do you think they won?

An English leader falls, and the English lose the Battle of Yorktown.

USING NEW WORDS

Complete the following sentences by using the words below.

British   fought   commander   battle   war

1. George Washington was the _____ of the colonial army.

2. The _____ ended in 1783.

3. The English soldiers lost the _____ at Yorktown.

4. The _____ is another name for the English.

5. The colonists _____ the English to gain independence.

SENTENCE COMPLETION

Think about what you have read and complete the sentences below.

1. George Washington is called "The Father of His Country" because ____

   _____.

2. When the English came to Lexington, _____

   _____.

3. Lexington and Concord are famous because _____

   _____.

4. At the battle of Yorktown, _____

   _____.

Answers for this chapter start on page 110.

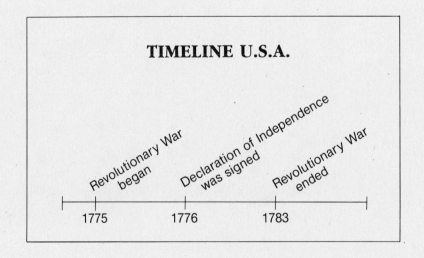

26

Chapter Review 1

WORD FIND

All of the words in the list are hidden in the box. They go from left to right and from top to bottom. Circle each one. One is done for you.

```
W  A  R  U  C  F  T  H  M
A  R  M  Y  O  B  P  O  Z
S  E  T  T  L  E  R  L  V
O  L  A  N  O  V  O  I  I
L  I  X  Q  N  P  T  D  L
D  G  S  X  Y  S  E  A  L
I  I  G  O  O  D  S  Y  A
E  O  R  I  G  H  T  S  G
R  N  S  H  I  P  V  W  E
```

✔ VILLAGE
SETTLER
COLONY
SHIP
RELIGION
SOLDIER
TAX
PROTEST
RIGHTS
HOLIDAYS
GOODS
ARMY
WAR

TIMELINE

Write the events in the correct order on the timeline. One of them is done for you.

~~Boston Tea Party~~
Columbus came to the Americas
Declaration of Independence
Plymouth colony was established

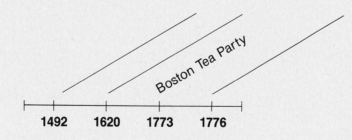

Boston Tea Party

1492   1620   1773   1776

MAP ACTIVITY

Label the original 13 colonies on this map. Use the arrows drawn to the colonies that are too small to write on. Look back at page 21 if you need help.

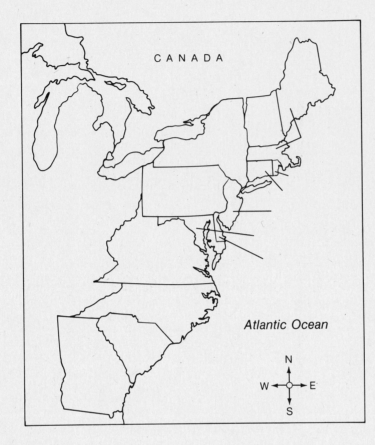

1. Connecticut
2. Delaware
3. Georgia
4. Maryland
5. Massachusetts
6. New Hampshire
7. New Jersey
8. New York
9. North Carolina
10. Pennsylvania
11. Rhode Island
12. South Carolina
13. Virginia

QUIZ

Find a partner and practice answering these questions.

1. Who was Christopher Columbus?

2. What were the first two English settlements?

3. Who were the Pilgrims?

4. What happened at the Boston Tea Party?

5. In 1776, how many colonies made up the United States?

6. Who wrote the Declaration of Independence?

7. On what day do we celebrate our nation's birthday?

8. Name the war in which the U.S. won independence from England.

9. Who was the great leader of this war?

10. Who was the first president of the United States?

Answers for this chapter review start on page 110.

Chapter 7
The Birth of the
Constitution

The U.S. Constitution was approved at the Constitutional Convention.

BEFORE YOU READ

1. Think about your native country. Is it divided into states, provinces, or other regions?

2. What is a federal government? What is a state government?

3. What is a congress?

4. What is a law? Give some examples of laws in your city or state in the United States.

5. What is a constitution? Does every country have one?

The Beginning of the U.S. Government

After the Revolution, the Continental Congress tried to form a new government. (A congress is a group of representatives. It meets to make laws.) To start this government, the Congress prepared the Articles of Confederation. The Articles were a collection of laws to govern all the colonies together.

As time passed, the Articles of Confederation did not work. The Articles gave too much independence to each individual state. The government of the whole United States was weak. It could not tax its citizens to raise money for the government. It could not defend the country in times of war. States could not trade with each other.

As a result, the Continental Congress decided to replace the Articles of Confederation. The Congress decided to plan a different form of government.

In 1787, the representatives had a convention, or meeting, in Philadelphia. George Washington was the leader of this convention. At the convention, the representatives wrote the Constitution of the United States. Two years later, in 1789, the Constitution was approved.

The Constitution explained the most basic and important laws of the U.S. government. It defined the powers of the federal and state governments, the judicial (legal) system, and the president.

After 1789, many more basic laws were added to the Constitution. In fact, there are many recent additions since the year 1900. However, today's Constitution is still basically the same as the original Constitution. It is still the highest law of the land.

WORDS TO KNOW
federal
law
power
Constitution
convention

AFTER YOU READ

Circle True (T) or False (F).

T F **1.** The Articles of Confederation were an early form for American laws.

T F **2.** Under the Articles of Confederation, the federal government was too weak.

T F **3.** The Constitution made the federal government stronger.

T F **4.** The Constitution was created in 1781.

T F **5.** The Constitution is the highest law of the land.

THINK ABOUT THE CONTINENTAL CONGRESS AND THE CONSTITUTION

Answer the following questions.

1. Who approved the Articles of Confederation?
2. What were some problems with the Articles of Confederation?
3. What happened at the convention in 1787?
4. What does the Constitution tell about?
5. Why is it good that laws can be added to the Constitution?

We the People of the United States, in order to form a more perfect Union, establish Justice, insure domestic Tranquility, provide for the common defence, promote the general Welfare, and secure the Blessings of Liberty to ourselves and our Posterity, do ordain and establish this Constitution for the United States of America.

"We the people"	Everyone is involved in the government.
"establish justice"	Everyone obeys the law,
"insure domestic tranquility"	keeps the peace,
"provide for the common defense"	protects the country, and
"promote the general welfare"	works for good government for all the people.
"secure the blessings of liberty to ourselves and our posterity"	We must always work to be free and to pass this liberty on to our children.

The Preamble, or introduction, to the Constitution has these important ideas.

USING NEW WORDS

Complete the following sentences by using the words below.

Constitution   federal   Articles of Confederation
laws   Philadelphia

1. An early plan for American government was the

   _____.

2. The convention met in _____.

3. The _____ government is the nation's government.

4. People must obey the _____ of their country.

5. The U.S. _____ is the highest law of the land.

SENTENCE COMPLETION

Think about what you read and complete the following sentences.

1. After the Revolution, the Continental Congress _____

   _____.

2. The representatives were not happy with the Articles of Confederation

   because _____

   _____.

3. At the convention in Philadelphia, the representatives _____

   _____.

4. The Constitution is important because _____

   _____.

Answers for this chapter start on page 111.

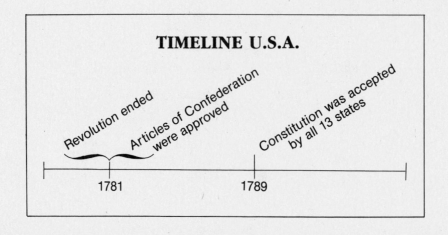

Chapter 8
The American Flag

The American flag has 50 stars for the 50 states.

BEFORE YOU READ

1. What does the flag of your native country look like?

2. What colors are on your native country's flag?

3. What does the American flag look like?

4. What colors are on the American flag?

5. In what public places do you see the American flag?

The Flag and the Pledge of Allegiance

Like all countries, the United States has a flag. But the American flag has changed over the years. The story of the changes in the flag is interesting.

George Washington was the commander of the American army during the Revolutionary War. An old story says that he asked a woman named Betsy Ross to make a flag.

Betsy Ross sewed a flag that had three colors: red, white, and blue. She put 13 white stars in a circle on a blue background. She also made 13 stripes representing the colonies. Seven stripes were red and six were white.

Since George Washington's time, the flag has changed. The red and white stripes are the same, but the pattern of the stars is different. A new star was added to the flag for every new state that became a part of the United States.

Today, there are 50 stars to stand for the 50 states in the United States. The 50 stars are now arranged in rows on a blue background. The 13 red and white stripes still represent the original colonies. Because of its design, the flag is often called the "Stars and Stripes."

The Pledge of Allegiance to the flag is usually recited, or said, with the right hand over the heart:

I pledge allegiance to the flag of the United States of America and to the republic for which it stands, one Nation under God, indivisible, with liberty and justice for all.

WORDS TO KNOW

stars
stripes
states
pledge
liberty
justice

AFTER YOU READ

Circle True (T) or False (F).

T   F   **1.** The American flag is red, white, and green.

T   F   **2.** George Washington sewed the first flag.

T   F   **3.** The first flag had 13 stars and 13 stripes.

T   F   **4.** Today there are 50 stars in the American flag.

T   F   **5.** People usually say the Pledge of Allegiance with their right hands over their hearts.

THINK ABOUT THE AMERICAN FLAG

Answer the following questions.

1. Who sewed the first flag?
2. Why were there 13 stars on the first flag?
3. Why are there 50 stars on the flag today?
4. Why are there still 13 stripes on the flag today?
5. Why do many Americans put a flag outside their houses on the Fourth of July and other national holidays?

The original flag had 13 stars for the 13 colonies.

35

USING NEW WORDS

Complete the following sentences by using the words below.

stars   justice   pledge   sewed   stripes

1. The American flag has 50 _____.

2. Betsy Ross _____ the first American flag.

3. The American government promises liberty and _____ to all.

4. The flag has red and white _____.

5. "I _____ allegiance to the flag of the United States of America. . . ."

SENTENCE COMPLETION

Think about what you have read and complete the sentences.

1. The first flag had 13 stars and 13 stripes because _____

   _____.

2. The first flag had 13 stars, but today's flag _____

   _____.

3. The flag has 50 stars because _____

   _____.

4. When a person says the pledge of allegiance, he or she usually _____

   _____.

Answers for this chapter start on page 111.

TIMELINE U.S.A.

Declaration of Independence was signed

First U.S. flag was created

Revolutionary War ended

1776   1777   1783

Chapter 9
The War of 1812 and the "Star-Spangled Banner"

Francis Scott Key saw the American flag flying over Fort McHenry.

BEFORE YOU READ

1. What is the national anthem (song) of your native country?

2. Is there a story about the flag of your native country?

3. What is the national anthem of the United States?

4. When can you hear the national anthem of the United States?

5. Think about the years after the Revolutionary War. Do you think that England and the U.S. had good or bad relations?

The War of 1812 and the National Anthem

England and France were at war in 1790. During the war, the United States sold products to the French. This made England angry, so England took action against the United States.

England acted against American ships. At that time, many sailors on U.S. ships were English. England began to stop American ships and take the English workers off of them. These English citizens had to fight in the war against France.

Sometimes the English also took American citizens, and this made the United States angry. There were now bad feelings between the two countries.

These bad feelings caused the War of 1812. The war lasted from 1812 to 1814. During this time, the Americans and the English fought battles on the Atlantic Ocean and in North America. The English burned the White House and the Capitol building in Washington, D.C.

On the night of September 13, 1814, the English navy attacked Fort McHenry, which was in the state of Maryland. An American man, Francis Scott Key, was watching the battle. It was raining hard, so Key could not see very well. He did not know if the United States was winning or losing the battle.

However, the next morning, he saw that the American flag was still flying over Fort McHenry. This showed that the Americans had not lost the fight. The Americans had defended themselves against the English.

Key was inspired, and he wrote a poem. It became known as the "Star-Spangled Banner." It is now the national song, or anthem, of the United States. People often sing this anthem at sporting events, such as baseball or football games, and at other special events.

WORDS TO KNOW	PEOPLE TO KNOW	PLACES TO KNOW
sailors flag anthem "Star-Spangled Banner"	Francis Scott Key	Fort McHenry Maryland

AFTER YOU READ

Circle True (T) or False (F).

T   F   **1.** England was at war with France in 1790.

T   F   **2.** The English were angry because the Americans helped France.

T   F   **3.** The War of 1812 was between England and France.

T   F   **4.** English soldiers burned the White House in the War of 1812.

T   F   **5.** The "Star-Spangled Banner" was written in 1790.

THINK ABOUT THE WAR OF 1812

Answer the following questions.

1. During the war with France, England was angry with the U.S. Why?
2. Why did the English take their citizens from American ships?
3. Where did the War of 1812 take place?
4. What inspired Francis Scott Key to write the "Star-Spangled Banner"?
5. Which two wars did the United States fight against England?

Star-Spangled Banner

Oh say, can you see, by the dawn's early light,
What so proudly we hailed at the twilight's last gleaming?
Whose broad stripes and bright stars, through the perilous fight,
O'er the ramparts we watched, were so gallantly streaming!
And the rockets' red glare, the bombs bursting in air,
Gave proof through the night that our flag was still there.
Oh say, does that star-spangled banner yet wave
O'er the land of the free and the home of the brave?

USING NEW WORDS

Complete the following sentences by using the words below.

citizen   **flag**   **anthem**   **White House**   **sailors**

1. If you were born in the U.S., you are a U.S. _____.

2. _____ are people who work on ships.

3. The U.S. _____ is red, white, and blue.

4. English soldiers burned the _____ and the Capitol.

5. The "Star-Spangled Banner" is the national _____.

SENTENCE COMPLETION

Think about what you have read and complete the sentences below.

1. England stopped American ships because _____

_____.

2. From 1812 to 1814, the United States _____

_____.

3. English soldiers invaded Washington, and they _____

_____.

4. The "Star-Spangled Banner" is the national anthem, and people _____

_____.

Answers for this chapter start on page 112.

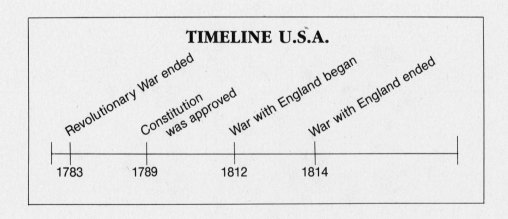

TIMELINE U.S.A.

Revolutionary War ended   Constitution was approved   War with England began   War with England ended

1783   1789   1812   1814

Chapter 10
Abraham Lincoln and the Civil War

Harriet Tubman, at the left, helped many slaves escape to freedom.

BEFORE YOU READ

1. What is a civil war? How is it different from other kinds of war?

2. Why is a civil war hard for a country?

3. Who fought in the American Civil War?

4. What is a slave? Where did most slaves in the United States come from?

5. Who was Abraham Lincoln?

A Nation Divided and a President Lost

Abraham Lincoln was born on February 12, 1809. Lincoln's family lived on a farm in the state of Kentucky, and they were very poor. Lincoln worked hard at different jobs to help his family. Lincoln loved books, and he often walked a long way to find books to read.

Lincoln became president of the United States in 1861. At that time, some Americans still owned slaves. Slaves were people from Africa who were forced to come to the United States and work. They did not get any money for this work. They were bought and sold like property.

Most Northern states wanted slavery to be illegal. However, most Southern states wanted to keep slavery because slaves were very important to the economy of the South. In the South, slaves worked in the tobacco and cotton fields.

To keep slavery, the Southern states decided to separate from the rest of the country. They wanted to make their own separate nation.

Finally, the North and the South went to war against each other. The Civil War lasted from 1861 to 1865. More than half a million people died in this war.

Abraham Lincoln wanted to keep the United States together as one nation. He also was against slavery. In 1863, Lincoln signed an important document. It was called the Emancipation Proclamation. The Emancipation Proclamation freed the slaves in the Southern states. Two years later, the war ended. The North had won.

The Civil War years were an emotional time in the United States, and some people hated Abraham Lincoln. In April 1865, an assassin shot and killed President Lincoln.

WORDS TO KNOW	PEOPLE TO KNOW	PLACES TO KNOW
slave slavery Civil War Emancipation Proclamation	Abraham Lincoln	Kentucky Africa the North the South

AFTER YOU READ

Circle True (T) or False (F).

T   F   1. Abraham Lincoln came from a poor family.

T   F   2. People from Africa wanted to come to the U.S. as slaves.

T   F   3. The South wanted slavery to be ended.

T   F   4. In the Civil War, the North wanted to form a separate nation.

T   F   5. The North won the Civil War.

THINK ABOUT ABRAHAM LINCOLN AND THE CIVIL WAR

Answer the following questions.

1. Why did the Southern states want to form their own nation?

2. Why did many people in the South support the use of slavery?

3. When did the Civil War begin and end?

4. How did Abraham Lincoln die?

5. Why do you think Abraham Lincoln signed the Emancipation Proclamation?

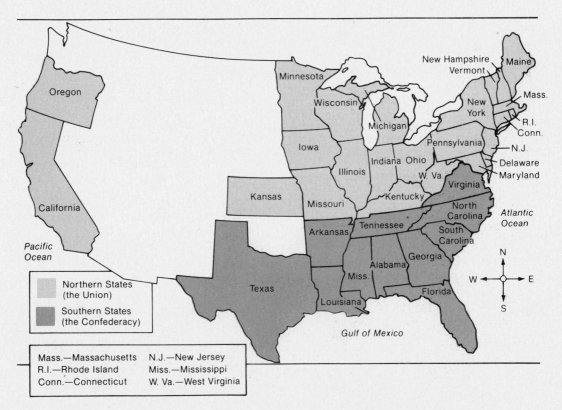

This map shows how the United States was divided during the Civil War.

43

USING NEW WORDS

Complete the following sentences by using the words below.

killed   slavery   cotton   free   separate

1. Abraham Lincoln was against _____.

2. In the South, slaves worked in the _____ fields.

3. The Southern states wanted to _____ from the rest of the country.

4. The slaves wanted to be _____.

5. An assassin _____ President Lincoln.

SENTENCE COMPLETION

Think about what you have read and complete the sentences below.

1. Lincoln came from a poor family, but he _____

_____.

2. The North wanted to keep the U.S. as one nation, but the South _____

_____.

3. In 1865, the North _____

_____.

4. In April 1865, an assassin _____

_____.

Answers for this chapter start on page 112.

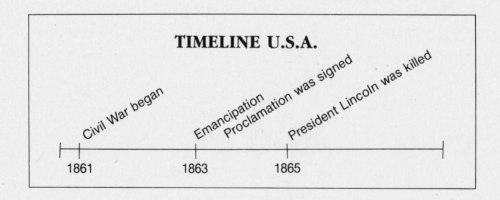

44

Chapter 11
Expansion and
Immigration

Many immigrants came to the United States to start a new life.

BEFORE YOU READ

1. Why do people come to live in the United States?

2. Where do you think most immigrants come from today?

3. Do you know where immigrants came from in the past?

4. Do you know why immigrants came here in the past?

5. Today there are 50 states in the United States. Were there always 50 states?

The Expansion of the United States

At the end of the 1700s, the territory of the United States extended west from the Atlantic Ocean to the Mississippi River. Then, in 1803, France sold a huge area of land to the United States.

The new territory reached west from the Mississippi to the Rocky Mountains. It included the areas between Canada and the Gulf of Mexico. This land was called the Louisiana Purchase. It almost doubled the size of the United States. In other words, the United States was now two times as big as it was before.

In 1848, after a war with Mexico, the United States took the land between the Rocky Mountains and the Pacific Ocean. The United States now extended all the way from the Atlantic Ocean to the Pacific Ocean.

In 1845, the Republic of Texas became part of the United States. Texas is the second largest state in the United States. The largest state is Alaska. Russia sold Alaska to the United States in 1867.

As the United States grew, there were more and more cities. More people left their farms and moved to the cities. They were looking for jobs. For the same reason, more immigrants came to the cities in the United States.

In the 1800s, most of these immigrants came from Europe. In fact, from 1820 to 1970, 36 million people came to the United States from Germany, Italy, Greece, and other European countries.

Today, some immigrants still come from Europe, especially Eastern European countries like Poland. However, more and more immigrants are coming from countries outside of Europe. They come from Latin American countries like Mexico, Guatemala, and Colombia, and from Asian countries like the Philippines and Korea. People come to this country for economic, political, and personal reasons.

WORDS TO KNOW	PLACES TO KNOW
Louisiana Purchase immigrants	Atlantic Ocean Pacific Ocean Mississippi River Texas Rocky Mountains Alaska

AFTER YOU READ

Circle True (T) or False (F).

T   F   **1.** The Louisiana Purchase doubled the size of the United States.

T   F   **2.** After the war with Mexico, U.S. territory reached to the Pacific Ocean.

T   F   **3.** In the 1800s, most immigrants came from Europe.

T   F   **4.** France sold Alaska to the United States.

T   F   **5.** Many of the new immigrants come to the United States from Asia.

THINK ABOUT THE EXPANSION OF THE UNITED STATES

Answer the following questions.

1. What land was included in the Louisiana Purchase?
2. After the war with Mexico, how far did the U.S. extend?
3. What are the two largest states in the U.S.?
4. As territory was added to the U.S., more and more immigrants came here. Why?
5. Think about immigrants of the past and present. In the past, where were most immigrants from? Today, where are they from?

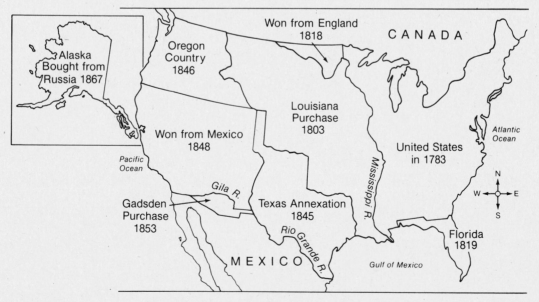

The expansion of the U.S. from 1783 to 1867.

47

USING NEW WORDS

Complete the following sentences by using the words below.

economic   territory   extends   immigrants   political

1. Today, the U.S. _____ from the Atlantic to the Pacific.

2. After the war with Mexico, the _____ of the United States extended to the Pacific Ocean.

3. Many _____ have come to live in the United States.

4. Some people come to the U.S. to escape their governments. They come for _____ reasons.

5. Some people come to the U.S. to get jobs. They come for _____ reasons.

SENTENCE COMPLETION

Think about what you have read and complete the following sentences.

1. Before the Louisiana Purchase, the territory of the United States extended from _____

   _____.

2. After the Louisiana Purchase, the United States _____

   _____.

3. In 1867, Russia _____

   _____.

4. As the United States grew, _____

   _____.

Answers for this chapter start on page 113.

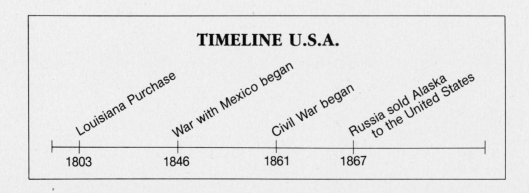

Chapter 12
The United States in the World Wars

These soliders are saying good-bye to their loved ones as they go off to war.

BEFORE YOU READ

1. Why have two wars been called world wars?

2. When was World War I? When was World War II?

3. Do you know who fought in these wars? Did your native country fight in these wars?

4. Were these wars fought on American land?

5. Think about the power of the U.S. in the world. Do you think the U.S. was stronger or weaker after the world wars?

The United States and the World Wars

There have been two world wars. World War I lasted from 1914 to 1918. World War II lasted from 1939 to 1945. These two wars began in Europe, but the United States fought in both.

In World War I, a group of nations including England and France went to war against a group of nations including Germany and Austria-Hungary. At first, the United States did not want to fight in this war. The American people believed the United States should not fight in wars so far away.

However, German warships attacked American ships in 1917, and the United States finally entered the war. The United States helped England and France win World War I. When the war ended in 1918, the U.S. had great economic and political power.

In World War II, a group of nations including England, the United States, and the Soviet Union fought against Germany, Italy, and Japan. The war began in 1939, but the U.S. did not enter the war at that time.

The United States entered this war in 1941. On December 7, 1941, Japanese planes bombed Pearl Harbor in Hawaii. More than 2,000 Americans died. The next day, the United States began to fight.

In May of 1945, Germany surrendered, or quit, but Japan continued to fight. During the war, the United States had built the first atomic bomb. The U.S. dropped two atomic bombs on Japan in August of 1945. The bombs killed hundreds of thousands of people. Japan surrendered, and World War II was over.

After this war, there were many political changes around the world. One of the changes was the new position of the United States. The United States had become one of the strongest and most powerful nations. As a result, American culture and influence began to affect countries around the world.

WORDS TO KNOW	PLACES TO KNOW
world	Germany
surrendered	Austria-Hungary
powerful	Soviet Union
World War I	Japan
World War II	

AFTER YOU READ

Circle True (T) or False (F).

T   F   **1.** There have been three world wars.

T   F   **2.** At first, the United States wanted to stay out of World War I.

T   F   **3.** The United States entered World War I in 1914.

T   F   **4.** After Pearl Harbor, Americans entered World War II.

T   F   **5.** The United States used the atomic bomb against Japan.

THINK ABOUT THE WORLD WARS

Answer the following questions.

1. Why did the U.S. enter World War I?

2. Why did the U.S. enter World War II?

3. In World War II, what countries fought on the same side as the U.S.?

4. In August 1945, what did the U.S. do to Japan?

5. After the world wars, how did the position of the U.S. change?

The United States entered World War II after the bombing of Pearl Harbor.

USING NEW WORDS

Complete the following sentences by using the words below.

atomic bomb   surrendered   power   fought   Germany

1. Germany stopped fighting, or _____, in 1945.

2. World War II ended when the Americans dropped the

   _____ on Japan.

3. Germany and Japan _____ against England and the United

   States.

4. _____ was in World War I and World War II.

5. American _____ increased after World War II.

SENTENCE COMPLETION

Think about what you have read and complete the following sentences.

1. In 1917, the United States _____

   _____.

2. In 1941, the United States _____

   _____.

3. In 1945, the United States _____

   _____.

4. After the world wars, the United States _____

   _____.

Answers for this chapter start on page 113.

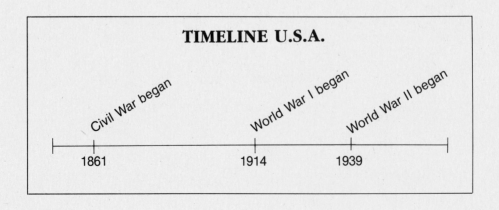

TIMELINE U.S.A.

Civil War began   World War I began   World War II began

1861   1914   1939

Chapter Review 2

WORD FIND

All of the words in the list are hidden in the box. They go from left to right and from top to bottom. Circle each one. One is done for you.

I	M	M	I	G	R	A	N	T
W	C	S	R	I	L	W	A	R
O	F	L	A	G	M	L	A	W
R	X	A	N	T	H	E	M	P
L	U	V	F	R	E	E	S	O
D	F	E	D	E	R	A	L	W
T	O	B	A	C	C	O	Y	E
S	U	R	R	E	N	D	E	R

✔FEDERAL
LAW
POWER
FLAG
ANTHEM
SLAVE
TOBACCO
FREE
IMMIGRANT
WORLD
SURRENDER
WAR

TIMELINE

Put the events in the correct order on the timeline.

U.S. Constitution was written
World War I began
World War II ended
Civil War ended

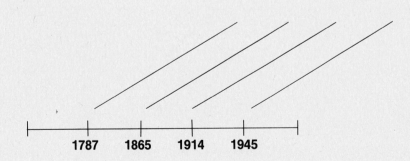

1787   1865   1914   1945

53

MAP ACTIVITY

On the map below, write the names of these places. Look back at page 47 if you need help.

1. Mexico
2. Canada
3. Mississippi River

4. Gulf of Mexico
5. Atlantic Ocean
6. Pacific Ocean

QUIZ

Find a partner and practice answering these questions.

1. What is the Constitution?

2. When was the Constitution adopted?

3. What is the "Star-Spangled Banner"?

4. Who wrote the "Star-Spangled Banner"?

5. What was the Civil War?

6. Who was the president during the Civil War?

7. Which side won the Civil War?

8. What happened to Lincoln after the Civil War ended?

9. Why did immigrants come to the United States in the late 1800s and the early 1900s?

10. Why did the United States enter World War II?

Answers for this chapter review start on page 114.

U.S. Government

These new U.S. citizens celebrate.

Chapter 13
What Is Democracy?

A man speaks out at a town meeting in his community.

BEFORE YOU READ

1. What is a citizen?

2. What is a democracy?

3. How does this picture show democracy in action?

4. What keeps a democracy strong?

5. Do you think that it is important to vote?

Democracy and Constitutional Rights

In the first 12 chapters of this book, we talked about the history of the United States. Now we will look at the government of the United States. Let's begin with some basic questions:

What is democracy?

Democracy is a type of government. In a democracy, the citizens control the government.

How do citizens control their government in a democracy?

In American democracy, citizens choose representatives in elections. In other words, they vote for representatives. These men and women become members of the government. If the citizens are not happy with their representatives, they can vote for new representatives at the next election.

What do representatives do?

The representatives make decisions for the citizens. These decisions should help to protect the rights of citizens.

What are rights?

The Constitution of the United States describes certain rights for all people. Some of the most important rights are the rights to:

- speak about anything
- believe in any religion
- own property
- not be cruelly punished by the government
- not go to prison without a fair trial in court

You will learn more about the Constitution in Chapters 14 through 20.

WORDS TO KNOW
democracy
citizens
elections
governments

AFTER YOU READ

Circle True (T) or False (F).

T   F   **1.** In a democracy, the citizens control the government.

T   F   **2.** In a democracy, people vote for representatives.

T   F   **3.** Citizens make decisions for the representatives.

T   F   **4.** The Constitution describes important rights.

T   F   **5.** In the United States, people must have the same religion.

THINK ABOUT DEMOCRACY

Answer the following questions.

1. Who elects representatives?

2. What do representatives do?

3. What can people do if they do not like their representatives?

4. What U.S. document describes the rights of the people?

5. What are some important rights described in the Constitution?

Democracy allows people to speak out for their rights.

59

USING NEW WORDS

Complete the following sentences by using the words below.

decisions   government   elections   right   protect

1. Citizens have the _____ to believe in any religion.

2. Representatives of the people are supposed to _____ certain rights.

3. In a democracy, the _____ is controlled by the people.

4. Citizens vote for representatives in _____.

5. Representatives make _____ for the people.

SENTENCE COMPLETION

Think about what you have read and complete the sentences below.

1. In a democracy, the citizens _____

_____.

2. If people do not like their representatives, they _____

_____.

3. The Constitution describes _____

_____.

4. People cannot go to prison without _____

_____.

Answers for this chapter start on page 114.

IN THE U.S.A. . . .

In the election for president in 1988, 89 million Americans
voted.

Chapter 14
The U.S. Constitution

Congress makes laws.

Judges explain laws.

BEFORE YOU READ

1. Why do governments have laws?

2. The U.S. Constitution is called "the highest law of the land." Why is this?

3. Do we use the Constitution today?

4. Is the Constitution today the same as the original?

5. What is the difference between a state government and the federal government?

An Introduction to the Constitution

More than 200 years ago, the United States became an independent nation. It had its own ideas about government. The people of the different states did not want a king. They did not want all the power in one part of the government. Instead, they wanted to divide the power.

The people wanted the federal government and the state governments to share power. They also wanted both large and small states to have power.

For these reasons, representatives of the states wrote the Constitution, the basic law of the nation. We still use the Constitution today, but it is longer than the original Constitution. Today's Constitution has three parts: the original Constitution, the Bill of Rights, and the other amendments. Let's look at each part now.

The original Constitution was written in 1787 and approved in 1789. It describes the relations between the federal government and the state governments. It divides the power of the federal government into three branches, or parts: the executive branch (president and vice president), the legislative branch (Congress), and the judicial branch (the courts).

The Bill of Rights was added in 1791. It is a list of 10 amendments, or additions, to the Constitution. It describes certain important rights.

Today's Constitution also has 16 other amendments. These amendments give more rights to the people. They were added after the Bill of Rights. The most recent amendment was added in 1971. In the future, the Constitution may have even more amendments.

In the next chapters, you will study the important parts of the Constitution in detail.

WORDS TO KNOW
Constitution original branch—branches Bill of Rights amendments

AFTER YOU READ

Circle True (T) or False (F).

T   F   **1.** Today's Constitution is exactly the same as the original Constitution.

T   F   **2.** Today's Constitution has five parts.

T   F   **3.** The original Constitution describes the relations between the federal and state governments.

T   F   **4.** An amendment is an addition to the Constitution.

T   F   **5.** The Bill of Rights is the first 10 amendments.

THINK ABOUT THE U.S. CONSTITUTION

Answer the following questions.

1. What are the three parts of the Constitution today?

2. What are the three branches of the U.S. government?

3. When was the Bill of Rights added?

4. The Bill of Rights has 10 amendments. How many other amendments are there?

5. It is hard to make changes in the Constitution. Why is this good?

Federal Government	State Governments
• makes national laws • rules on important court cases • directs relations with other countries • distributes money to the states	• support local schools • build highways and prisons • look after public health • provide welfare for the poor

These are some of the duties of the federal government and of state governments.

USING NEW WORDS

Complete the following sentences by using the words below.

original   Constitution   branches   relations   Bill of Rights

1. The _____ is the basic law of the land.

2. The _____ Constitution was approved in 1789.

3. The _____ is the first 10 amendments.

4. There are three _____ of the U.S. government.

5. The Constitution describes the _____ among the states.

SENTENCE COMPLETION

Think about what you have read and complete the sentences below.

1. The Constitution is the _____.

2. Today's Constitution is made up of _____.

3. The original Constitution describes the relations between _____

   _____.

4. The Bill of Rights is a list of _____

   _____.

Answers for this chapter start on page 115.

IN THE U.S.A. . . .

The United States Constitution is the oldest constitution in the world.

64

Chapter 15
Three Branches of
U.S. Government

Former President John F. Kennedy speaking to Congress and the Supreme Court.

BEFORE YOU READ

1. In your native country, who is the most powerful person in the government?

2. How can someone become the leader of a government?

3. What are the three branches of government in the United States?

4. Do you think one branch is more important than the others?

5. Why do you think there are three branches?

The Three Branches of Government

In the United States, power is not controlled by just one area of the government. Different parts of the government share the power.

The men who wrote the Constitution did not want the president to be as powerful as the king of England. They were afraid that a president would control the United States. But they did not want the Congress to be too strong, either. They wanted to balance the power in the government.

The writers of the Constitution decided to create three areas, or branches, of government. Each branch of government would have different kinds of power, and no branch would have too much power.

One branch of the U.S. government is the executive branch. This includes the president and the vice president. It also includes other departments that help the president. The executive branch works to put laws into effect.

Another branch of government is the legislative branch. This includes the two houses of Congress: the Senate and the House of Representatives. The Congress makes new laws.

The third branch of government is the judicial branch. The judicial branch is the court system. The courts explain laws and punish people who break the law. The most important court in the United States is the Supreme Court.

The three branches must work together in U.S. government. In the next chapters, you will study each branch.

WORDS TO KNOW

balance
executive branch
judicial branch
legislative branch
Supreme Court

AFTER YOU READ

Circle True (T) or False (F).

T   F   **1.** There are four branches of government.

T   F   **2.** The judicial branch makes new laws.

T   F   **3.** The Senate is part of the legislative branch.

T   F   **4.** The executive branch includes the president and the vice president.

T   F   **5.** The executive branch has more power than the legislative branch.

THINK ABOUT THE THREE BRANCHES OF GOVERNMENT

Answer the following questions.

1. Why did the writers of the Constitution want three different branches of government?

2. What does the executive branch do?

3. What does the legislative branch do?

4. What does the judicial branch do?

5. What would happen if one branch of government got too much power?

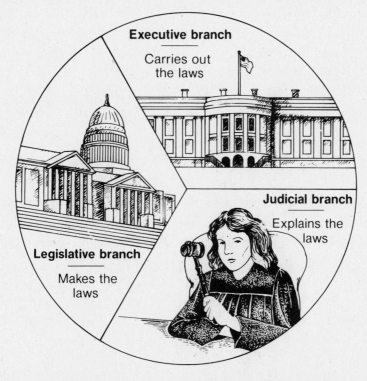

The three branches of government work together.

USING NEW WORDS

Complete the following sentences by using the words below.

Supreme Court   punish   legislative   executive   balance

1. The Constitution tries to _____ power in the government.

2. The _____ branch creates laws.

3. The judicial branch has the power to _____ people who break the law.

4. The vice president is in the _____ branch.

5. The judicial branch includes the _____.

SENTENCE COMPLETION

Think about what you have read and complete the sentences below.

1. The executive branch includes _____
_____.

2. The legislative branch includes _____
_____.

3. The judicial branch includes _____
_____.

4. The three branches must _____
_____.

Answers for this chapter start on page 115.

IN THE U.S.A. . . .

The three branches of government have some control over each other. For instance, the president and the Senate have power to choose the judges of the Supreme Court. But the Supreme Court has the power to say that laws made by Congress and the president are illegal.

Chapter 16
The Executive Branch

The president of the United States lives and works in the White House.

BEFORE YOU READ

1. Who is the president or leader of your native country?

2. Who were some of the most famous U.S. presidents? Who is the president now?

3. What does the president do?

4. What do you think are characteristics of a good president?

5. If something happens to the president, who takes his place?

The Executive Branch

The executive branch of the U.S. government has three parts: the president, the vice president, and the president's cabinet. (The cabinet is a group of people that helps the president.) The president is the head, or leader, of the executive branch. He lives and works in the White House in Washington, D.C.

Every four years, American citizens elect a president and a vice president. A president can be elected only two times.

In many ways, the president is the most important person in the U.S. government. He has many responsibilities. He must approve laws made by Congress. He is the commander of the military, and he maintains relations with other countries. His decisions affect the entire United States.

The vice president is another important person in the government. If the president dies or quits, the vice president becomes the new president. The vice president is also the head of the Senate. If necessary, he can vote in the Senate to break a tie vote.

The cabinet helps the president with his responsibilities. The cabinet has 14 members. Most members are called secretaries, and each one is in charge of a different area of government. For example, there is a secretary of defense, a secretary of state, a secretary of labor, and so on.

The president, the vice president, and the cabinet work together to carry out the responsibilities of the executive branch of government.

WORDS TO KNOW

elect
president
vice president
commander
cabinet
secretary—secretaries

AFTER YOU READ

Circle True (T) or False (F).

T   F   **1.** A person can be president for 12 years.

T   F   **2.** If something happens to the president, the vice president takes his place.

T   F   **3.** The vice president can vote in the Senate.

T   F   **4.** There are eight cabinet members in the president's cabinet.

T   F   **5.** Most of the cabinet members are called secretaries.

THINK ABOUT THE EXECUTIVE BRANCH

Answer the following questions.

1. What are the three important parts of the executive branch?
2. What does the president do?
3. What does the vice president do?
4. What do the cabinet members do?
5. Why do you think a president can be elected only two times?

The 41st president of the United States is George Bush.

USING NEW WORDS

Complete the following sentences by using the words below.

   vice president elect executive responsibilities cabinet

1. The president is the head of the _____ branch of government.

2. Every four years, people _____ a president.

3. The _____ can take the place of the president.

4. The president has 14 _____ members to help him.

5. Cabinet members help the president with his _____.

SENTENCE COMPLETION

Think about what you have read and complete the sentences below.

1. The three parts of the executive branch are _____

 _____.

2. Every four years, citizens elect _____

 _____.

3. If the president dies, _____

 _____.

4. Three examples of cabinet members are the secretary of defense, _____

 _____.

Answers for this chapter start on page 116.

IN THE U.S.A. . . .

There have been 41 presidents of the United States. Eight vice presidents have had to lead the nation after the death of a president. The first cabinet was created by George Washington. There were three cabinet members at that time.

Chapter 17
The Legislative Branch

Former Mexican President José Lopez Portillo addresses the U.S. Congress.

BEFORE YOU READ

1. Do you know the names of the senators in your state?

2. What is the legislative branch of the national government?

3. What does the legislative branch do?

4. How do people become members of the legislative branch?

5. Where does the legislative branch work?

The Legislative Branch

The legislative branch of the U.S. government is the Congress of the United States. Its job is to make laws for the nation.

All of the states have representatives in the U.S. Congress. Congress has two parts, or "houses": the Senate and the House of Representatives. Both houses are located in the Capitol building in Washington, D.C.

In the Senate, each state has two representatives. They are called senators. Each state has equal power in the Senate because it has the same number of senators as the other states. There are 50 states, so there is a total of 100 senators. Senators serve terms of six years.

In the House of Representatives, there are 435 representatives. Each state has a different number of representatives, depending on its population. States with many people have more representatives—and power—than states with few people. For example, in 1988 Texas had 27 representatives, and Alaska had only one. Representatives serve terms of two years.

Both the Senate and the House of Representatives make laws for the United States. Let's see how the laws are made. First, Congress creates a bill. A bill is an idea for a new law. If both houses of Congress approve the bill, they send the bill to the president. If the president likes the bill, he signs it. Then the bill becomes a law. If he doesn't sign it, he may send it back to Congress.

As you can see, the legislative branch must work together with the executive branch in order to make new laws. The judicial branch makes sure that laws follow the Constitution. In this way, all three branches work together.

WORDS TO KNOW

Congress
House of Representatives
Senate
senator
Capitol building
bill

AFTER YOU READ

Circle True (T) or False (F).

T F 1. The legislative branch makes the laws.

T F 2. There are two houses in the Senate.

T F 3. Each state has the same number of senators.

T F 4. Each state has the same number of representatives.

T F 5. Both houses of Congress and the president must accept a
          bill before it becomes law.

THINK ABOUT THE LEGISLATIVE BRANCH

Answer the following questions.

1. What are the two houses of Congress?
2. How long is the term of a senator? How long is the term of a
   representative?
3. Why do we have 100 senators?
4. Why does Texas have more representatives than Alaska?
5. Do you think that it is good that the president is involved in approving
   laws? Why?

	Senators	Representatives
How many are there?	100	435
How many from each state?	2 senators	It depends on how many people live in the state.
How long are their terms?	6 years	2 years
How old must they be?	30 years old	25 years old

This chart shows the differences between senators and representatives.

USING NEW WORDS

Complete the following sentences by using the words below.

Congress   senator   Representatives   legislative   laws

1. _____ has two houses.

2. The term of a _____ is six years.

3. The U.S. House of _____ is located in the

   Capitol building.

4. The _____ branch of government creates laws.

5. The houses of Congress work together to create _____.

SENTENCE COMPLETION

Think about what you have read and complete the sentences below.

1. One house of Congress is the House of Representatives, and the other

   house is _____.

2. Some states have more representatives than others because _____

   _____.

3. The number of representatives is different in every state, but the number

   of senators _____.

4. When a bill goes to the president, he can _____

   _____.

Answers for this chapter start on page 116.

IN THE U.S.A. . . .

   The Senate gives all states the same number of senators. The
   House gives larger states more representatives. The creation of
   the two houses is called the "Great Compromise."

Chapter 18
The Judicial Branch

The Supreme Court of the United States is made up of nine judges called justices.

BEFORE YOU READ

1. Have you ever been in a court? Tell about your experience.

2. Why are courts necessary?

3. What do judges do?

4. What do you think are important characteristics of a good judge?

5. Which is the most important court in the United States?

The Judicial Branch

The judicial branch of government is a system of courts. These courts have two jobs: to interpret, or explain, the laws and to enforce the laws.

There are many different kinds of courts. For example, there are criminal courts and traffic courts. But the most important court in the United States is the Supreme Court. The Supreme Court judges examine laws, and they decide if the Constitution permits the laws. All other courts must obey the decisions of the Supreme Court.

There are nine judges on the Supreme Court. These judges decide on important legal problems. To do this, they meet and vote. A majority of judges (five or more) must agree on a decision. Then the decision is final.

The Supreme Court is located in Washington, D.C. The members of the Supreme Court can keep their jobs for life. The president chooses new Supreme Court judges, but the Senate must approve the new judge. This is a good example of how powers are shared by the executive, legislative, and judicial branches of the government.

WORDS TO KNOW
judicial
courts
interpret
enforce
judge

AFTER YOU READ

Circle True (T) or False (F).

T F **1.** The legislative branch interprets and enforces laws.

T F **2.** The highest court in the U.S. is the Supreme Court.

T F **3.** There are 20 judges on the Supreme Court.

T F **4.** Citizens vote for Supreme Court judges in national elections.

T F **5.** The Supreme Court makes sure that laws agree with the Constitution.

THINK ABOUT THE JUDICIAL BRANCH

Answer the following questions.

1. How does a person become a member of the Supreme Court?
2. How long can a Supreme Court judge serve?
3. What does the Supreme Court do?
4. How does the Supreme Court make decisions?
5. Why is the Supreme Court located in Washington, D.C.?

Two children sit in front of the Supreme Court building. The Supreme Court has made many decisions to guarantee equal education for Americans of all races.

USING NEW WORDS

Complete the following sentences by using the words below.

judges   judicial   interprets   chooses   courts

1. The Supreme Court is part of the _____ branch of government.

2. The judicial branch is a system of _____.

3. The Supreme Court _____ laws.

4. There are nine _____ on the Supreme Court.

5. The president _____ the members of the Supreme Court.

SENTENCE COMPLETION

Think about what you have read and complete the sentences below.

1. The highest court is _____.

2. The Supreme Court decides if _____

   _____.

3. The president selects a new judge for the Supreme Court, but the

   Senate _____

   _____.

4. The judicial branch is one branch of the U.S. government. The other

   branches _____

   _____.

Answers for this chapter start on page 117.

IN THE U.S.A. . . .

The Senate has rejected presidents' choices for new Supreme
Court judges 27 times. In 1987, the Senate rejected Judge
Robert Bork, who was chosen by President Reagan.

Chapter Review 3

WORD FIND

All of the words in the list are hidden in the box. They go from left to right and from top to bottom. Circle each one. One is done for you.

```
D  B  A  L  A  N  C  E  B        ✓BALANCE
E  J  U  D  G  E  F  Z  R         CABINET
M  P  R  O  T  E  C  T  A         BILL
O  L  B  I  L  L  I  C  N         LAWS
C  A  B  I  N  E  T  O  C         JUDGE
R  W  V  Y  P  C  I  U  H         COURT
A  S  Q  T  U  T  Z  R  V         DEMOCRACY
C  C  H  O  O  S  E  T  T         CITIZEN
Y  R  I  G  H  T  N  U  R         ELECT
                                  PROTECT
                                  RIGHT
                                  CHOOSE
                                  BRANCH
```

FIND OUT

Find out the names of these officials and write them down. Practice saying each name.

1. The president of the U.S.: _____

2. The vice president: _____

3. The senators from your state: _____

   and _____

4. The governor of your state: _____

5. Your congressman (the person who represents you in the House of

   Representatives): _____

MATCH-UP

Listed below are things that each branch of government does. Put each phrase in the correct box.

EXECUTIVE

1. _____
2. _____
3. _____

writes new laws

punishes people who break
  the law

LEGISLATIVE

1. _____
2. _____
3. _____

runs the military

makes sure laws are obeyed

has senators and representatives

explains the laws

includes the cabinet

JUDICIAL

1. _____
2. _____
3. _____

makes sure that laws agree with the
  Constitution

has two parts, or houses

QUIZ

Find a partner and practice answering these questions.

1. What is the form of government in the U.S.?

2. How many branches are there in the U.S. government?

3. What does each branch do?

4. What are the two parts of Congress?

5. How many members are in the House of Representatives?

6. What is the term of office for a person in the House of Representatives?

7. How many members are there in the Senate?

8. What is the term of office for a U.S. senator?

9. What is the term of office for the president of the U.S.?

10. Who takes the president's place if he cannot finish his term?

11. How many times can a person be elected president?

12. What is the name of the highest court in the land?

13. Who picks the judges on this court?

14. How long can the judges serve?

15. Where is this court located?

Answers for this chapter review start on page 117.

Chapter 19
The Bill of Rights

The Bill of Rights guarantees Americans the right to a fair trial.

BEFORE YOU READ

1. The Bill of Rights is part of the Constitution. What do we mean by rights?

2. What rights do you think are in the Constitution?

3. What rights are gained when a person becomes a permanent resident? And what rights are gained when a person becomes a citizen?

4. Do you think it's important for a government to write down people's rights? Why?

5. The picture shows a trial in court. What could happen if a person is arrested and doesn't have the right to a fair trial?

The Bill of Rights: the First 10 Amendments

The United States Constitution was adopted in 1789, but we still use it today. Why do we use such an old document?

The Constitution is still used because we can add new laws to it. Additions to the Constitution are called amendments. It is hard to create an amendment. In 200 years, only 26 amendments have been added.

In 1791, 10 famous amendments were added to the Constitution. These amendments are called the Bill of Rights. The Bill of Rights helps to protect the liberty of people in the United States.

The Bill of Rights says that in the United States:

- a person can talk or write about anything he wants
- a person can believe in any or no religion
- a person must have a trial in a court if the government says that he has broken a law
- a person can have a lawyer if he has to go to court
- a person must receive a fair, quick trial in court

The Bill of Rights also says that:

- the government cannot go into a person's house without special permission
- the government cannot be cruel to a person who has broken the law

These are only some of the more famous rights and liberties protected by the Bill of Rights.

WORDS TO KNOW

amendments
Bill of Rights
liberty
trial
court

AFTER YOU READ

Circle True (T) or False (F).

T   F   **1.** We can change the Constitution by adding amendments.

T   F   **2.** The first 12 amendments are called the Bill of Rights.

T   F   **3.** It is easy to add amendments to the Constitution.

T   F   **4.** The Bill of Rights says that the government cannot be cruel to citizens who have broken the law.

T   F   **5.** The Bill of Rights is part of the original Constitution.

THINK ABOUT THE BILL OF RIGHTS

Answer the following questions.

1. What do we call a new law added to the Constitution?

2. What is the Bill of Rights?

3. When was the Bill of Rights adopted?

4. What are some of the rights in the Bill of Rights?

5. Which rights do you think are most important? Why?

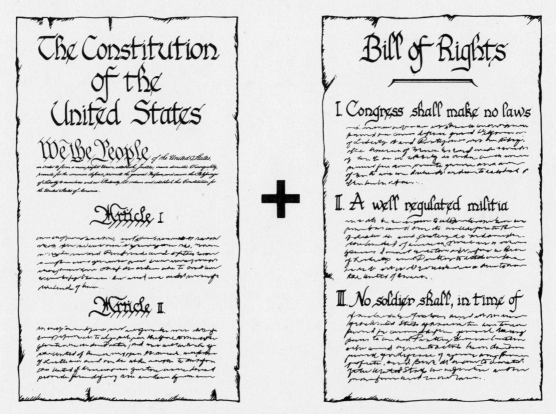

Together, the Constitution and the Bill of Rights are the basis of
American government and freedoms.

USING NEW WORDS

Complete the following sentences using the words below.

court liberties trial cruel amendments

1. A person has the right to a fair _____ in court.

2. The Constitution can be changed by adding _____.

3. A person has a right to a trial in a _____.

4. The Bill of Rights helps to protect _____.

5. The Bill of Rights says that the government cannot be _____ to a

 person.

SENTENCE COMPLETION

Think about what you have read and complete the sentences below.

1. To change the Constitution, _____

 _____.

2. The Bill of Rights is _____

 _____.

3. The Bill of Rights says that a person can talk _____

 _____.

4. The government cannot enter people's houses if it does not have _____

 _____.

Answers for this chapter start on page 118.

IN THE U.S.A. . . .

  The United States Bill of Rights is one of the world's three
  famous bills of rights:
  English Bill of Rights, 1689
  French Declaration of the Rights of Man and of the Citizen,
   1789
  United States Bill of Rights, 1791

Chapter 20
Other Amendments

These women marched to gain the right to vote.

BEFORE YOU READ

1. If the Constitution is the highest law, why can it be changed?

2. What word is used to describe changes made to the Constitution?

3. What is the name of the first 10 amendments to the Constitution?

4. Who do you think can add an amendment to the Constitution? (The president? The Supreme Court? The Congress? The citizens?)

5. The women in the picture marched for the right to vote. How do you think women got that right?

Amending the Constitution

The Bill of Rights, the first 10 amendments to the Constitution, was created in 1791. Since then, 16 other amendments have been added. There are now 26 amendments.

It is not easy to add an amendment to the Constitution. Usually, both houses of the U.S. Congress must approve the amendment. Two-thirds (2/3) of each house must vote for it. Then the state congresses (these are called legislatures or assemblies) must approve the amendment. Three-fourths (3/4) of the 50 state congresses must vote for it.

It is difficult to get so many votes. That is why only 26 amendments have been added in the last 200 years. The most recent amendment was in 1971, and it permits citizens to vote when they are 18 years old.

Now let's look at some more of the amendments in detail. Several amendments give more rights to the people. Some of these amendments include the following:

Amendment 13 (1865)—slavery is ended

Amendment 19 (1920)—women can vote

Amendment 24 (1964)—no one has to pay a tax to vote for members of Congress or the president

Amendment 26 (1971)—citizens 18 years old or older can vote

Other amendments help the government function, or work, better. Here are two examples:

Amendment 16 (1913)—Congress has the right to tax the money people earn

Amendment 22 (1951)—a person cannot be president more than twice.

WORDS TO KNOW
amendment
approve

AFTER YOU READ

Circle True (T) or False (F).

T   F   **1.** There are 26 amendments to the Constitution.

T   F   **2.** There cannot be any more amendments in the future.

T   F   **3.** Women did not always have the right to vote in the United States.

T   F   **4.** Before 1971, 18-year-old citizens could not vote.

T   F   **5.** It is easy to add an amendment.

THINK ABOUT THE AMENDMENTS TO THE CONSTITUTION

Answer the following questions.

1. Who must approve a new amendment?

2. What did Amendment 13 do?

3. Which amendments make it easier for people to vote?

4. Which amendment gave the government more money?

5. Which of the amendments do you think is the most important?

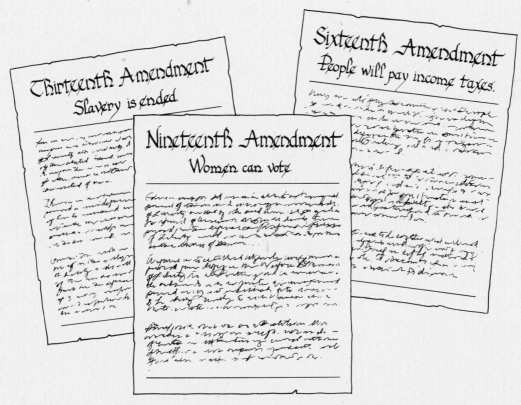

Altogether, there are 26 amendments to the U.S. Constitution.

USING NEW WORDS

Complete the following sentences by using the words below.

taxes   slavery   amendment   function   rights

1. The Twenty-second _____ says that the president can serve only two terms.

2. Some amendments give more _____ to people.

3. The Thirteenth Amendment put an end to _____.

4. As a result of the Sixteenth Amendment, Americans had to pay more _____.

5. Some amendments help the government to _____ better.

SENTENCE COMPLETION

Think about what you have read and complete the sentences below.

1. Amendment 19 says that _____

   _____.

2. The newest amendment is _____

   _____.

3. Amendment 26 says that _____

   _____.

4. I believe the most important amendment is Amendment _____,

   because _____.

Answers for this chapter start on page 118.

IN THE U.S.A. . . .

In 1972, the U.S. Congress approved an amendment. It said that women and men should have the same rights. However, this "Equal Rights Amendment" was not approved by three-fourths of the states, so it was not added to the Constitution.

Chapter 21
The Voting Process

U.S. citizens can vote in local, state, and national elections.

BEFORE YOU READ

1. What happens in an election?

2. How old must a person be to vote in the United States?

3. Do you know the two major political parties in the United States?

4. Is the president a Republican or a Democrat?

5. Do you want to vote in elections in the United States? Why?

Voting and Elections

There have been elections in North America since the time of the colonists. At first, not everyone could vote. For example, in the past, men could vote but women could not.

However, the situation is different today. There have been several amendments to the Constitution about voting. The Constitution now gives voting rights to black people, women, and 18-year-olds.

Citizens can vote in three basic types of elections: national, state, and local. There are national elections for the president and vice president. There are state elections for governors, senators, and other officials. And there are local elections for leaders such as mayors.

In an election, there are usually two or more candidates. A candidate is someone who wants to be elected. For instance, in 1988, George Bush and Michael Dukakis were the candidates for president. Candidates are usually members of a political party.

The largest political parties in the United States are the Democratic Party and the Republican Party. These two parties have different ideas about government and how government should work. People can vote for candidates of either party.

To be able to vote, a person must be a citizen of the United States. The person must be at least 18 years old on the day of the election. He or she must also be a registered voter. Different states have different laws about registration. Usually, a citizen can register to vote at the offices of his or her community government.

WORDS TO KNOW

candidates
Democratic Party
citizen
political party
Republican Party
register

AFTER YOU READ

Circle True (T) or False (F).

T F 1. If you want to vote, you must be at least 21 years old.

T F 2. Black people and women have always been able to vote in the United States.

T F 3. If people want to vote, they must register to vote.

T F 4. Only citizens can vote.

T F 5. There are three large political parties in the United States.

THINK ABOUT VOTING AND ELECTIONS

Answer the following questions.

1. What are the major political parties in the United States?

2. Who can vote in the United States?

3. Why are there amendments about voting in the Constitution?

4. What are the three basic kinds of elections?

5. Why do you think a person has to be registered to vote?

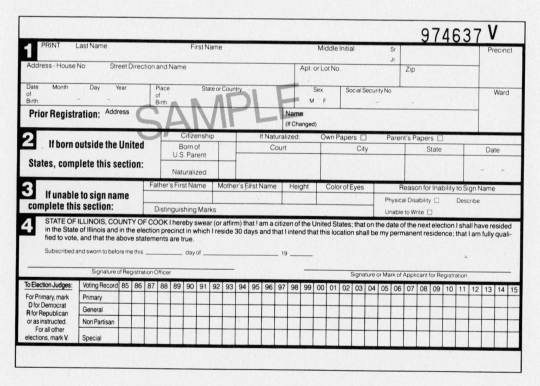

Before citizens can vote, they must register.

USING NEW WORDS
Complete the following sentences by using the words below.

candidates   citizens   registered   national   parties

1. Citizens must be _____ before they can vote.

2. There are two major political _____ in the United States.

3. People vote for _____ in an election.

4. The president is elected in a _____ election.

5. _____ who are 18 years old have the right to vote.

SENTENCE COMPLETION
Think about what you have read and complete the sentences below.

1. In national elections, people vote for _____

_____.

2. In state elections, people vote _____

_____.

3. In local elections, people _____

_____.

4. If a person wants to vote, _____

_____.

Answers for this chapter start on page 119.

IN THE U.S.A. . . .
Candidates in elections are usually members of one of two major political parties. These political parties choose their candidates in special elections called primaries.

Chapter Review 4

WORD FIND

All of the words in the list are hidden in the box. They go from left to right and from top to bottom. Circle each one. One is done for you.

K	A	F	C	R	U	E	L	S
M	M	L	F	T	L	Y	A	R
L	E	A	A	D	D	P	W	I
I	N	G	V	O	T	E	Y	G
B	D	C	O	U	R	T	E	H
E	M	P	A	R	T	Y	R	T
R	E	G	I	S	T	E	R	S
T	N	A	T	I	O	N	A	L
Y	T	R	I	A	L	P	O	R

✓ AMENDMENT
  LIBERTY
  TRIAL
  COURT
  CRUEL
  REGISTER
  VOTE
  NATIONAL
  PARTY
  FLAG
  LAWYER
  RIGHTS
  ADD

MATCH-UP

Match each holiday to the correct date. If you need help, look at the calendar on page 106.

_____ 1. Memorial Day
_____ 2. Independence Day
_____ 3. Thanksgiving
_____ 4. Christmas
_____ 5. Labor Day
_____ 6. Columbus Day
_____ 7. Lincoln's Birthday
_____ 8. New Year's Day

a. January 1
b. February 12
c. last Monday in May
d. July 4
e. first Monday in September
f. second Monday in October
g. fourth Thursday in November
h. December 25

QUIZ

Find a partner and practice answering these questions.

1. Can the Constitution be changed?

2. How many amendments does the Constitution have?

3. What is the Bill of Rights?

4. What are two rights guaranteed by the Bill of Rights?

5. What are some other important amendments?

6. What are the requirements for voting?

7. What are the two major political parties?

Answers for this chapter review start on page 119.

Appendix 1

Commonly Asked Questions About U.S. History

1. What were the people who settled Plymouth called?
2. What holiday began with the Pilgrims?
3. Where were the first English settlements?
4. What was the Boston Tea Party?
5. Who was the first commander-in-chief of the American army?
6. How many original colonies became the United States?
7. How many original colonies can you name?
8. What is the Declaration of Independence?
9. What are the basic rights set forth in the Declaration of Independence?
10. Who wrote the Declaration of Independence?
11. On what date did the members of the Continental Congress meet to vote on the Declaration of Independence?
12. Who was the first president of the United States?
13. When is his birthday?
14. Who is called "The Father of His Country"?
15. What is the birthdate of the United States?
16. Why do we celebrate the Fourth of July?
17. Who was president when the Civil War was fought?
18. Name five states that belonged to the Union (the North).
19. Name five states that belonged to the Confederacy (the South).
20. What happened to Lincoln after the Civil War ended?
21. Which side won the Civil War?
22. What is the "Star-Spangled Banner"?
23. Who wrote the "Star-Spangled Banner"?
24. How did the writer of the "Star-Spangled Banner" feel about his country?
25. Name the first, third, and sixteenth presidents of the United States.

Answers to Questions About U.S. History

1. The people who settled Plymouth were called **Pilgrims**.

2. **Thanksgiving** began with the Pilgrims.

3. The first English settlements were in **Jamestown, Virginia**, and in **Plymouth, Massachusetts**.

4. In Boston, Massachusetts, **colonists dressed as Indians went on English ships and threw the cargo of tea into the water**. They did this to show they were unhappy with the tax.

5. The first commander of the American army was **George Washington**.

6. **Thirteen** original colonies became the United States.

7. The first 13 colonies were: **Connecticut, Delaware, Georgia, Maryland, Massachusetts, New Hampshire, New Jersey, New York, North Carolina, Pennsylvania, Rhode Island, South Carolina, and Virginia**.

8. The Declaration of Independence is **a document that declared our independence from England**.

9. The Declaration of Independence says that all people have the right to **life, liberty, and the pursuit of happiness**.

10. **Thomas Jefferson** wrote the Declaration of Independence.

11. **July 4, 1776**, was the date the members of the Continental Congress met to vote on the Declaration of Independence.

12. **George Washington** was the first president of the United States.

13. His birthday is **February 22**.

14. The "Father of His Country" is **George Washington**.

15. The birthdate of the United States is the **Fourth of July**, or **Independence Day**.

16. We celebrate the Fourth of July **to remember our independence from England**.

17. The president of the United States during the Civil War was **Abraham Lincoln**.

18. The states that belonged to the Union, or the North, were: **California, Connecticut, Delaware, Illinois, Indiana, Iowa, Kansas, Kentucky, Maine, Massachusetts, Michigan, Minnesota, Missouri, New Hampshire, New Jersey, Ohio, Oregon, Pennsylvania, Rhode Island, Vermont, West Virginia, and Wisconsin**.

19. The states that belonged to the Confederacy, or the South, were: **Alabama, Arkansas, Florida, Georgia, Louisiana, Mississippi, North Carolina, South Carolina, Tennessee, Texas, and Virginia**.

20. **Lincoln was shot** on April 15, 1865, one week after the Civil War ended, by a man who loved the South.

21. **The Union, or the North**, won the Civil War.

22. The "Star-Spangled Banner" is our **national anthem**, or song.

23. It was written by **Francis Scott Key**.

24. Francis Scott Key felt **very patriotic, or loyal**, to his country.

25. The first president was **George Washington**, the third president was **Thomas Jefferson**, and the sixteenth president was **Abraham Lincoln**.

Appendix 2

Commonly Asked Questions About U.S. Government

1. What is the highest law of the land?
2. What is the Constitution?
3. When was the Constitution adopted?
4. What is the form of government in the United States?
5. What is a republic?
6. Can the Constitution be changed?
7. How many amendments does the Constitution have?
8. What is the Bill of Rights?
9. What are two of the rights guaranteed by the Bill of Rights?
10. What are some of the important amendments that are not in the Bill of Rights?
11. How many branches of government does the United States have? What are they?
12. What does the legislative branch do?
13. How many parts is Congress divided into? Name them.
14. How many members are there in the House of Representatives?
15. For how many years is a representative elected?
16. What is the name of your representative in Congress?
17. How many members are there in the Senate?
18. For how many years is a senator elected?
19. What are the names of your senators?
20. How many senators are elected from each state?
21. What does the judicial branch do?
22. What is the name of the highest court in the United States? How many judges (justices) are on this court?
23. Who picks the judges on this court?
24. How long can these judges serve?
25. Where is this court located?
26. What does the executive branch do?
27. Who is the leader of the executive branch?
28. Who is the president of the United States?
29. For how many years is a United States president elected?
30. How many times can a person be elected president of the United States?
31. What are the qualifications needed to be president of the United States?
32. Who takes the president's place if he cannot finish his time in office?
33. Who is the vice president of the United States?
34. What is the Cabinet?
35. How many presidents has the United States had to this date?

36. Can the president be removed from office? How?
37. How many states are in the United States?
38. What is the capital of the United States?
39. What are three basic requirements that allow a person to vote?
40. What are the two major political parties in the United States?
41. What political party does President Bush belong to?
42. Describe the American flag today.
43. What colors are on the American flag?
44. Describe the first American flag.
45. What legal holiday is February 12?
46. What legal holiday is July 4?
47. What legal holiday is November 11?
48. Who is the governor of your state?
49. Where is your state capital?
50. Who is the mayor of your city or town?

Answers to Questions About U.S. Government

1. The **Constitution** is the highest law of the land.

2. The Constitution is **a legal document that tells the rights of the citizens and the powers of the federal government.**

3. The Constitution was adopted in **1789.**

4. The form of government in the United States is called a **democracy**, or a democratic republic.

5. A republic is a government in which the **people are governed by leaders whom they have elected.**

6. Changes can be made in the Constitution by **amendments.**

7. The Constitution now has **26** amendments. This includes the Bill of Rights.

8. The Bill of Rights is the **first 10 amendments** to the Constitution.

9. Some of the rights guaranteed by the Bill of Rights are: **freedom of speech, freedom of the press, freedom of religion, the right to peaceful assembly**, and **the right to a fair trial.**

10. Some other important amendments are:

    a. 13th: **no more slavery**

    b. 19th: **women can vote**

    c. 22nd: **the president can only be elected twice**

    d. 26th: **lowered the minimum voting age to 18**

11. The United States government has **three branches**. They are the **legislative, judicial, and executive**.

12. The legislative branch **makes the laws**.

13. Congress is divided into **two parts**. They are the **Senate** and the **House of Representatives**.

14. There are **435 members** in the House of Representatives.

15. A representative is elected for a **two-year term**.

16. The name of my representative is (answers will vary).

17. There are **100** members in the Senate.

18. A senator is elected for a **six-year** term.

19. My two senators are (answers will vary).

20. **Two senators** are elected from each state.

21. The judicial branch **interprets the laws**, or says what they mean.

22. The **Supreme Court** is the highest court in the United States. There are **nine judges** (justices) on the Supreme Court.

23. The **president** picks the Supreme Court judges.

24. These judges can serve **for life**.

25. The Supreme Court is in **Washington, D.C.**

26. The executive branch **enforces the laws**.

27. The **president** is the leader of the executive branch.

28. The president of the United States is **George Bush**.

29. The president of the United States is elected for a **four-year term**.

30. A person can be elected president of the United States **two times**.

31. To be president of the United States, you must be at least **35 years old, a 14-year resident of the United States, and born in the United States**.

32. The **vice president** would take the president's place.

33. The vice president of the United States is **Dan Quayle**.

34. The Cabinet is **14 secretaries of different departments** picked by the president to help him make decisions.

35. The United States has had **41 presidents**.

36. **Yes**, the president can be removed from office. He can be removed by **impeachment, trial, and conviction**.

37. There are **fifty states** in the United States.

38. **Washington, D.C.**, is the capital of the United States.

39. A person must be at least **18 years old, a citizen of the United States**, and **registered to vote** in his or her state at least 30 days before the election.

40. The two major political parties in the United States are the **Democratic Party and the Republican Party.**

41. President Bush belongs to the **Republican Party.**

42. The American flag has **13 red-and-white stripes and 50 white stars on a blue background.**

43. The colors on the American flag are **red, white, and blue.**

44. The first American flag had **13 red-and-white stripes and 13 white stars on a blue background.**

45. **Lincoln's Birthday** is the holiday on February 12.

46. July 4 is **Independence Day**, or the nation's birthday.

47. November 11 is called **Veterans Day**. It honors the men and women who served in the military.

48. The governor of my state is (answers will vary).

49. The state capital is (answers will vary).

50. The mayor is (answers will vary).

Appendix 3

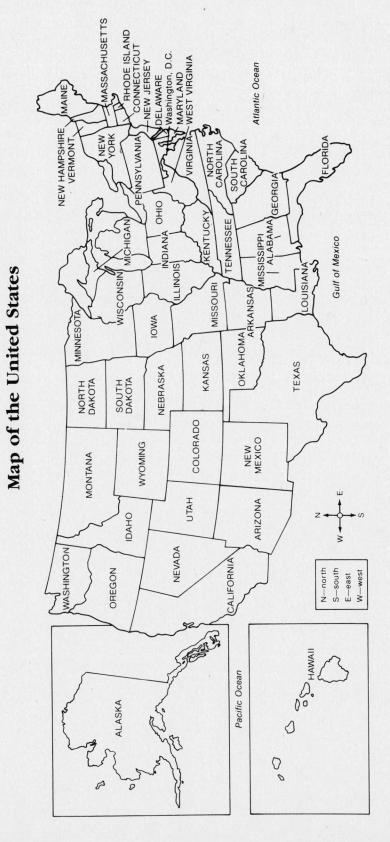

Map of the United States

Appendix 4

The States and Their Capitals

State	Abbreviation	Capital
Alabama	AL	Montgomery
Alaska	AK	Juneau
Arizona	AZ	Phoenix
Arkansas	AR	Little Rock
California	CA	Sacramento
Colorado	CO	Denver
Connecticut	CT	Hartford
Delaware	DE	Dover
Florida	FL	Tallahassee
Georgia	GA	Atlanta
Hawaii	HI	Honolulu
Idaho	ID	Boise
Illinois	IL	Springfield
Indiana	IN	Indianapolis
Iowa	IA	Des Moines
Kansas	KS	Topeka
Kentucky	KY	Frankfort
Louisiana	LA	Baton Rouge
Maine	ME	Augusta
Maryland	MD	Annapolis
Massachusetts	MA	Boston
Michigan	MI	Lansing
Minnesota	MN	St. Paul
Mississippi	MS	Jackson
Missouri	MO	Jefferson City
Montana	MT	Helena
Nebraska	NE	Lincoln
Nevada	NV	Carson City
New Hampshire	NH	Concord
New Jersey	NJ	Trenton
New Mexico	NM	Santa Fe
New York	NY	Albany
North Carolina	NC	Raleigh
North Dakota	ND	Bismarck

State	Abbreviation	Capital
Ohio	OH	Columbus
Oklahoma	OK	Oklahoma City
Oregon	OR	Salem
Pennsylvania	PA	Harrisburg
Rhode Island	RI	Providence
South Carolina	SC	Columbia
South Dakota	SD	Pierre
Tennessee	TN	Nashville
Texas	TX	Austin
Utah	UT	Salt Lake City
Vermont	VT	Montpelier
Virginia	VA	Richmond
Washington	WA	Olympia
West Virginia	WV	Charleston
Wisconsin	WI	Madison
Wyoming	WY	Cheyenne

Appendix 5

1989

Months

January

February

March

April

May

June

July

August

September

October

November

December

Days of the Week

Sunday (Su)

Monday (M)

Tuesday (Tu)

Wednesday (W)

Thursday (Th)

Friday (F)

Saturday (Sa)

	S	M	T	W	T	F	S
JAN.	①2	3	4	5	6	7	
	8	9	10	11	12	13	14
	15	⑯	17	18	19	20	21
	22	23	24	25	26	27	28
	29	30	31				

	S	M	T	W	T	F	S
FEB.				1	2	3	4
	5	6	7	8	9	10	11
	⑫	13	14	15	16	17	18
	19	20	21	㉒	23	24	25
	26	27	28				

	S	M	T	W	T	F	S
MAR.				1	2	3	4
	5	6	7	8	9	10	11
	12	13	14	15	16	17	18
	19	20	21	22	23	24	25
	26	27	28	29	30	31	

	S	M	T	W	T	F	S
APR.							1
	2	3	4	5	6	7	8
	9	10	11	12	13	14	15
	16	17	18	19	20	21	22
	23	24	25	26	27	28	29
	30						

	S	M	T	W	T	F	S
MAY		1	2	3	4	5	6
	7	8	9	10	11	12	13
	14	15	16	17	18	19	20
	21	22	23	24	25	26	27
	28	㉙	30	31			

	S	M	T	W	T	F	S
JUNE					1	2	3
	4	5	6	7	8	9	10
	11	12	13	14	15	16	17
	18	19	20	21	22	23	24
	25	26	27	28	29	30	

	S	M	T	W	T	F	S
JULY							1
	2	3	④	5	6	7	8
	9	10	11	12	13	14	15
	16	17	18	19	20	21	22
	23	24	25	26	27	28	29
	30	31					

	S	M	T	W	T	F	S
AUG.			1	2	3	4	5
	6	7	8	9	10	11	12
	13	14	15	16	17	18	19
	20	21	22	23	24	25	26
	27	28	29	30	31		

	S	M	T	W	T	F	S
SEPT.						1	2
	3	④	5	6	7	8	9
	10	11	12	13	14	15	16
	17	18	19	20	21	22	23
	24	25	26	27	28	29	30

	S	M	T	W	T	F	S
OCT.	1	2	3	4	5	6	7
	8	⑨	10	11	12	13	14
	15	16	17	18	19	20	21
	22	23	24	25	26	27	28
	29	30	31				

	S	M	T	W	T	F	S
NOV.			1	2	3	4	
	5	6	7	8	9	10	11
	12	13	14	15	16	17	18
	19	20	21	22	㉓	24	25
	26	27	28	29	30		

	S	M	T	W	T	F	S
DEC.						1	2
	3	4	5	6	7	8	9
	10	11	12	13	14	15	16
	17	18	19	20	21	22	23
	24	㉕	26	27	28	29	30
	31						

Holidays

New Year's Day—January 1

Martin Luther King, Jr., Day—January 16*
(Third Monday in January)

Lincoln's Birthday—February 12

Washington's Birthday—February 22

Memorial Day—May 29*
(Last Monday in May)

Fourth of July/Independence Day—July 4

Labor Day—September 4*
(First Monday in September)

Columbus Day—October 9*
(Second Monday in October)

Thanksgiving—November 23*
(Last Thursday in November)

Christmas—December 25

*These dates are different from year to year.

Appendix 6

United States Presidents (and years served)

1. George Washington (1789-1797)
2. John Adams (1797-1801)
3. Thomas Jefferson (1801-1809)
4. James Madison (1809-1817)
5. James Monroe (1817-1825)
6. John Q. Adams (1825-1829)
7. Andrew Jackson (1829-1837)
8. Martin Van Buren (1837-1841)
9. William Harrison (1841)
10. John Tyler (1841-1845)
11. James Polk (1845-1849)
12. Zachary Taylor (1849-1850)
13. Millard Fillmore (1850-1853)
14. Franklin Pierce (1853-1857)
15. James Buchanan (1857-1861)
16. Abraham Lincoln (1861-1865)
17. Andrew Johnson (1865-1869)
18. Ulysses Grant (1869-1877)
19. Rutherford Hayes (1877-1881)
20. James Garfield (1881)
21. Chester Arthur (1881-1885)
22. Grover Cleveland (1885-1889)
23. Benjamin Harrison (1889-1893)
24. Grover Cleveland (1893-1897)
25. William McKinley (1897-1901)
26. Theodore Roosevelt (1901-1909)
27. William Taft (1909-1913)
28. Woodrow Wilson (1913-1921)
29. Warren Harding (1921-1923)
30. Calvin Coolidge (1923-1929)
31. Herbert Hoover (1929-1933)
32. Franklin Roosevelt (1933-1945)
33. Harry Truman (1945-1953)
34. Dwight Eisenhower (1953-1961)
35. John Kennedy (1961-1963)
36. Lyndon Johnson (1963-1969)
37. Richard Nixon (1969-1974)
38. Gerald Ford (1974-1977)
39. Jimmy Carter (1977-1981)
40. Ronald Reagan (1981-1989)
41. George Bush (1989-   )

Answer Key

CHAPTER 1
NATIVE AMERICANS
After You Read
1. F   4. T
2. F   5. F
3. T

Think About Native Americans
Correct answers will vary.
1. The first people came to North America for food.
2. They walked across the small piece of land connecting Asia and North America.
3. Native Americans got their food by hunting animals.
4. Later, Native Americans got their food by raising animals and growing new plants.
5. Native Americans still live in North and South America.

Using New Words
1. continents   4. raised
2. hunted   5. Indians
3. settled

Sentence Completion
Correct answers will vary.
1. People came to North America from Asia because **they were looking for food.**
2. Hunters were people who **followed and killed animals to eat.**
3. Some groups did not have to travel for food, so **they stayed in one place and formed villages.**
4. Native Americans grew new plants such as **corn, tomatoes, and tobacco.**

CHAPTER 2
CHRISTOPHER COLUMBUS AND THE NEW WORLD
After You Read
1. F   2. F   3. T   4. F   5. T

Think About Columbus
Correct answers will vary.
1. People traveled from Europe to Asia by land.
2. Columbus thought that he could reach Asia by sailing across the ocean.
3. The Queen of Spain was rich and powerful.
4. Columbus thought that he had reached Asia.
5. The New World was found.

Using New Words
1. goods   4. valuable
2. round   5. New World
3. ships

Sentence Completion
Correct answers will vary.
1. Europeans went to Asia because **they could buy valuable goods there.**
2. Europeans traveled to Asia by land, but Columbus **tried to reach Asia by crossing the ocean.**
3. To help Columbus, the Queen of Spain **gave him three ships and men to sail with him.**
4. In 1492, Columbus tried to reach Asia, but **he reached the New World instead.**

CHAPTER 3
JAMESTOWN AND PLYMOUTH
After You Read
1. T   4. T
2. F   5. F
3. F

Think About Jamestown and Plymouth
Correct answers will vary.
1. The English formed Jamestown in 1607.
2. The Pilgrims came to North America for religious freedom.

3. The Pilgrims were hungry and sick, and many died.
4. The Pilgrims had a great celebration to give thanks for their food and health.
5. Thanksgiving Day is an important holiday in the United States because families come together and give thanks.

Using New Words

1. colonies
2. Jamestown
3. Plymouth
4. religious
5. Thanksgiving

Sentence Completion

Correct answers will vary.
1. Jamestown was the first **permanent English settlement.**
2. In 1607, people came to Jamestown, and in 1620 **the Pilgrims formed Plymouth colony.**
3. At first, life was difficult for the Pilgrims because **they were sick and had little food.**
4. Today, Thanksgiving is celebrated on **the fourth Thursday in November.**

CHAPTER 4
BEGINNINGS OF THE REVOLUTION
After You Read

1. T
2. F
3. T
4. T
5. F

Think About Rebellion in the Colonies

Correct answers will vary.
1. The colonists were under the control of the English government, and they did not like it.
2. Colonists protested in front of a government building.
3. Five (5) colonists died in the Boston Massacre.
4. The colonists threw tea into the harbor to protest against taxes.
5. The colonies were angry with the English.

Using New Words

1. tax
2. colonists
3. protested
4. guns
5. rebellion

Sentence Completion

Correct answers will vary.
1. The colonists were angry with England because **the English government controlled the colonies.**
2. A group of colonists went to a government building and **began to protest.**
3. During the Boston Massacre, the English soldiers **fired their guns at the protesters.**
4. During the Boston Tea Party, some colonists **threw tea into Boston Harbor.**

CHAPTER 5
THE DECLARATION OF INDEPENDENCE
After You Read

1. F
2. T
3. T
4. T
5. F

Think About the Declaration of Independence

Correct answers will vary.
1. There were 13 colonies in 1776.
2. The colonists wrote the Declaration to tell why they wanted to be independent.
3. Representatives of the 13 colonies approved the Declaration of Independence on July 4, 1776.
4. The Declaration of Independence talks about people's basic rights and the colonies as free and independent states.
5. The king was angry, and England went to war with the colonies.

Using New Words

1. rights
2. approved
3. representatives
4. Independence Day
5. independent

Sentence Completion

Correct answers will vary.

1. On July 4, 1776, representatives of the colonies **approved the Declaration of Independence**.
2. The Declaration of Independence says that **the colonies wanted to be free**.
3. The Declaration of Independence was written because **the colonies wanted to explain their desire for independence**.
4. July 4 is called the nation's birthday because **the Declaration of Independence was signed that day**.

CHAPTER 6
GEORGE WASHINGTON AND THE REVOLUTION
After You Read

1. T   4. F
2. F   5. T
3. T

Think About the American Revolution

Correct answers will vary.

1. The Revolutionary War began in 1775.
2. The Revolutionary War ended in 1783.
3. The colonies won the Revolutionary War.
4. The colonists no longer wanted to be controlled by England.
5. The colonists won because they were well prepared.

Using New Words

1. commander   4. British
2. war   5. fought
3. battle

Sentence Completion

Correct answers will vary.

1. George Washington is called "The Father of His Country" because **he was the first president and was the commander of the colonial army in the Revolutionary War**.

2. When the English came to Lexington, **they were surprised by the colonists**.
3. Lexington and Concord are famous because **the first battles of the Revolutionary War were fought there**.
4. At the battle of Yorktown, **George Washington's army won**.

CHAPTER REVIEW 1
Word Find

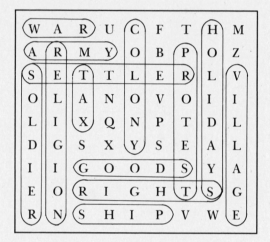

Timeline

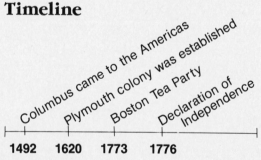

Map Activity

Check your answers against the map on page 21.

Quiz

1. Christopher Columbus was a European who found the New World in 1492.
2. The first English settlements were in Jamestown, Virginia, and in Plymouth, Massachusetts.
3. The people who settled Plymouth were called Pilgrims. They wanted religious freedom in the New World.

110

4. In 1773, colonists protested a tax on tea. They went to ships in Boston Harbor and threw the tea into the water.
5. There were 13 colonies that made up the United States.
6. Thomas Jefferson wrote most of the Declaration of Independence.
7. The birthdate is the Fourth of July, or Independence Day.
8. The Revolutionary War is the war in which the U.S. won independence from England.
9. The great leader of this war was George Washington.
10. The first president of the U.S. was George Washington.

CHAPTER 7
THE BIRTH OF THE CONSTITUTION
After You Read
1. T   4. F
2. T   5. T
3. T

Think About the Continental Congress and the Constitution
Correct answers will vary.
1. The Continental Congress approved the Articles of Confederation.
2. The federal government was too weak, and the states were too independent of each other.
3. The representatives wrote the Constitution of the United States.
4. The Constitution tells about the basic laws of the United States and the powers of the state and federal governments.
5. As times change, some laws must also change.

Using New Words
1. Articles of Confederation
2. Philadelphia
3. federal
4. laws
5. Constitution

Sentence Completion
Correct answers will vary.
1. After the Revolution, the Continental Congress **tried to form a national government. They approved the Articles of Confederation**.
2. The representatives were not happy with the Articles of Confederation because **they gave too much power to the individual states**.
3. At the convention in Philadelphia, the representatives **wrote the Constitution of the United States**.
4. The Constitution is important because **it explains the basic and most important laws of the United States government**.

CHAPTER 8
THE AMERICAN FLAG
After You Read
1. F   4. T
2. F   5. T
3. T

Think About the Flag
Correct answers will vary.
1. An old story says that Betsy Ross sewed the first flag.
2. There were 13 stars on the first flag because there were 13 original colonies.
3. There are 50 stars on the flag today because there are 50 states.
4. The 13 stripes represent the 13 original colonies.
5. Many Americans display the flag to show pride in their country on national holidays.

Using New Words
1. stars   4. stripes
2. sewed   5. pledge
3. justice

Sentence Completion
Correct answers will vary.
1. The first flag had 13 stars and stripes because **each star and each stripe stood for one of the colonies**.

2. The first flag had 13 stars, but today's flag **has 50 stars**.
3. The flag has 50 stars because **stars were added to the American flag when new states became part of the United States**.
4. When a person says the pledge of allegiance, he or she usually **puts the right hand over the heart**.

CHAPTER 9
THE WAR OF 1812 AND THE "STAR-SPANGLED BANNER"
After You Read
1. T
2. T
3. F
4. T
5. F

Think About the War of 1812
Correct answers will vary.
1. England became angry with the U.S. because the U.S. was selling products to the French.
2. The English took their citizens from American ships to force the citizens to fight against France.
3. The War of 1812 took place on the Atlantic Ocean and in North America.
4. The sight of the American flag still flying inspired Francis Scott Key to write the "Star-Spangled Banner."
5. In the Revolutionary War and the War of 1812, the United States fought against England.

Using New Words
1. citizen
2. Sailors
3. flag
4. White House
5. anthem

Sentence Completion
Correct answers will vary.
1. England stopped American ships because **there were English citizens on the ships**.
2. From 1812 to 1814, the United States **was at war with England**.

3. English soldiers invaded Washington, and they **set fire to the White House**.
4. The "Star-Spangled Banner" is the national anthem, and people **often sing it at public ceremonies**.

CHAPTER 10
ABRAHAM LINCOLN AND THE CIVIL WAR
After You Read
1. T
2. F
3. F
4. F
5. T

Think About Abraham Lincoln and the Civil War
Correct answers will vary.
1. The Southern states wanted to keep slavery.
2. Slaves worked in the cotton and tobacco fields.
3. The Civil War began in 1861 and ended in 1865.
4. Abraham Lincoln was shot and killed by an assassin.
5. The Emancipation Proclamation freed slaves in the South and made the South weaker.

Using New Words
1. slavery
2. cotton
3. separate
4. free
5. killed

Sentence Completion
Correct answers will vary.
1. Lincoln came from a poor family, but he **eventually became president of the United States**.
2. The North wanted to keep the U.S. as one nation, but the South **wanted to form a separate nation**.
3. In 1865, the North **won the Civil War**.
4. In April 1865, an assassin **shot and killed Abraham Lincoln**.

CHAPTER 11
EXPANSION AND IMMIGRATION
After You Read
1. T
2. T
3. T
4. F
5. T

Think About the Expansion of the United States
Correct answers will vary.
1. The Louisiana Purchase included land between the Mississippi River and the Rocky Mountains.
2. After the war with Mexico, the United States extended from the Atlantic Ocean to the Pacific Ocean.
3. The two largest states are Alaska and Texas.
4. As territory was added to the United States, more and more immigrants came to look for jobs.
5. In the past, most immigrants were from European countries. Today, most immigrants come from Mexico, Central and South America, and Asian countries.

Using New Words
1. extends
2. territory
3. immigrants
4. political
5. economic

Sentence Completion
Correct answers will vary.
1. Before the Louisiana Purchase, the territory of the United States extended from **the Atlantic Ocean west to the Mississippi River**.
2. After the Louisiana Purchase, the United States **was almost twice as big as it was before**.
3. In 1867, Russia **sold Alaska to the United States**.
4. As the United States grew, **immigration increased**.

CHAPTER 12
THE UNITED STATES IN THE WORLD WARS
After You Read
1. F
2. T
3. F
4. T
5. T

Think About the World Wars
Correct answers will vary.
1. The U.S. entered World War I in 1917 because German warships attacked American ships.
2. The United States entered World War II in 1941 because Japanese planes bombed Pearl Harbor.
3. In World War II, England and the Soviet Union fought on the same side as the U.S.
4. In August 1945, the United States dropped two atomic bombs on Japan.
5. After the world wars, the United States became a stronger and more powerful nation.

Using New Words
1. surrendered
2. atomic bomb
3. fought
4. Germany
5. power

Sentence Completion
Correct answers will vary.
1. In 1917, the United States **entered World War I**.
2. In 1941, the United States **entered World War II**.
3. In 1945, the United States **dropped two atomic bombs on Japan**.
4. After the world wars, the United States **became a strong and powerful nation that affected other countries around the world**.

CHAPTER REVIEW 2
Word Find

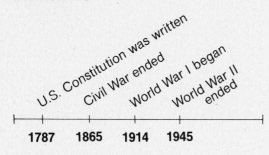

Timeline

U.S. Constitution was written
Civil War ended
World War I began
World War II ended

| 1787 | 1865 | 1914 | 1945 |

Map Activity

Check your answers against the map on page 47.

Quiz

1. The Constitution is the supreme law of the land. It defines the structure and powers of the federal government.
2. The Constitution was adopted in 1789.
3. The "Star-Spangled Banner" is our national song or anthem.
4. It was written by Francis Scott Key.
5. It was a war between the North and the South to free the slaves.
6. Abraham Lincoln was president during the Civil War.
7. The Union (the North) won the Civil War.
8. Lincoln was killed after the Civil War ended.
9. Immigrants came to have land and get jobs.
10. The U.S. entered World War II because Japan bombed Pearl Harbor.

CHAPTER 13
WHAT IS DEMOCRACY?
After You Read

1. T
2. T
3. F
4. T
5. F

Think About Democracy

Correct answers will vary.
1. The citizens elect representatives.
2. Representatives make decisions to protect the rights of citizens.
3. If people do not like their representatives, they can vote for new ones at the next election.
4. The Constitution describes the rights of the people.
5. Some of the most important rights are the rights to:
   speak about anything
   believe in any religion
   own property
   not be cruelly punished by the government
   not go to prison without a fair trial in court

Using New Words

1. right
2. protect
3. government
4. elections
5. decisions

Sentence Completion

Correct answers will vary.
1. In a democracy, the citizens **control the government**.
2. If people do not like their representatives, they **can vote for new representatives at the next election**.
3. The Constitution describes **certain rights for all people**.
4. People cannot go to prison without **a fair trial in court**.

114

CHAPTER 14
THE U.S. CONSTITUTION

After You Read

1. F
2. F
3. T
4. T
5. T

Think About the U.S. Constitution

Correct answers will vary.

1. The three parts of today's Constitution are the original Constitution, the Bill of Rights, and the other amendments.
2. The three branches of the U.S. government are the executive branch (president and vice president), the legislative branch (Congress), and the judicial branch (the courts).
3. The Bill of Rights was added in 1791.
4. There are 16 other amendments to the Constitution.
5. It is good that it is hard to change the Constitution because it should only be changed for an important reason.

Using New Words

1. Constitution
2. original
3. Bill of Rights
4. branches
5. relations

Sentence Completion

Correct answers will vary.

1. The Constitution is the **basic law of the nation**.
2. Today's Constitution is made up of **the original Constitution, the Bill of Rights, and the other amendments**.
3. The original Constitution describes the relations between **federal and state governments**.
4. The Bill of Rights is a list of **10 amendments that describes certain important rights**.

CHAPTER 15
THREE BRANCHES OF U.S. GOVERNMENT

After You Read

1. F
2. F
3. T
4. T
5. F

Think About the Three Branches of Government

Correct answers will vary.

1. The writers of the Constitution wanted three different branches so that the power in government would be balanced.
2. The executive branch works to put laws into effect.
3. The legislative branch creates new laws.
4. The judicial branch explains the laws and punishes people who break the law.
5. If one branch got too much power, it could force the whole government to do what it wanted.

Using New Words

1. balance
2. legislative
3. punish
4. executive
5. Supreme Court

Sentence Completion

Correct answers will vary.

1. The executive branch includes **the president, the vice president, and other departments that help the president**.
2. The legislative branch includes **the two houses of Congress: the Senate and the House of Representatives**.
3. The judicial branch includes **the court system**.
4. The three branches must **work together in our government**.

CHAPTER 16
THE EXECUTIVE BRANCH

After You Read

1. F
2. T
3. T
4. F
5. T

Think About the Executive Branch

Correct answers will vary.

1. The three important parts of the executive branch are the president, the vice president, and the president's cabinet.
2. The president approves laws made by Congress, is commander of the military, and maintains relations with other countries.
3. The vice president becomes the new president if the president dies or quits. He also is the head of the Senate and votes in the Senate, if necessary, to break a tie vote.
4. The cabinet members help the president with his responsibilities.
5. A president can only serve two times so that no individual can gain too much power.

Using New Words

1. executive
2. elect
3. vice president
4. cabinet
5. responsibilities

Sentence Completion

Correct answers may vary.

1. The three parts of the executive branch are **the president, the vice president, and the president's cabinet.**
2. Every four years, citizens elect **a president and a vice president.**
3. If the president dies, **the vice president becomes the new president.**
4. Three examples of cabinet members are the secretary of defense, **secretary of state, and secretary of labor.**

CHAPTER 17
THE LEGISLATIVE BRANCH

After You Read

1. T
2. F
3. T
4. F
5. T

Think About the Legislative Branch

Correct answers will vary.

1. The two houses of Congress are the Senate and the House of Representatives.
2. The term of a senator is six years. The term of a representative is two years.
3. We have 100 senators because there are 50 states and each state has two senators.
4. Texas has more representatives than Alaska because Texas has a larger population.
5. It is important that the president is involved in approving the laws because he is responsible for carrying out the laws.

Using New Words

1. Congress
2. senator
3. Representatives
4. legislative
5. laws

Sentence Completion

Correct answers will vary.

1. One house of Congress is the House of Representatives, and the other house is **the Senate.**
2. Some states have more representatives than others because **the number of representatives is based on population.**
3. The number of representatives is different in every state, but the number of senators **is the same for every state.**
4. When a bill goes to the president, he can **sign it if he likes it.**

CHAPTER 18
THE JUDICIAL BRANCH
After You Read

1. F   4. F
2. T   5. T
3. F

Think About the Judicial Branch

Correct answers will vary.
1. A person becomes a member of the Supreme Court when the president chooses him or her and the Senate approves of him or her.
2. A Supreme Court judge can serve for life.
3. The Supreme Court examines laws and decides if the Constitution permits them.
4. The Supreme Court votes to make decisions. A majority of judges must agree on the decision.
5. Answers will vary. A possible answer is that Washington, D.C., is the capital of the U.S.

Using New Words

1. judicial
2. courts
3. interprets
4. judges
5. chooses

Sentence Completion

Correct answers will vary.
1. The highest court is **the Supreme Court.**
2. The Supreme Court decides if **the Constitution permits a law.**
3. The president selects a new judge for the Supreme Court, but the Senate **must approve the new judge.**
4. The judicial branch is one branch of the U.S. government. The other branches **are the executive and the legislative.**

CHAPTER REVIEW 3
Word Find

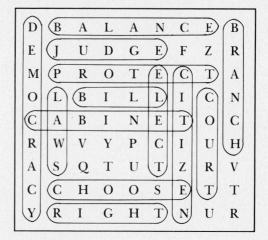

Find Out

Your teacher can give you the correct answers.

Match-up

Executive
1. runs the military
2. makes sure laws are obeyed
3. includes the cabinet

Legislative
1. writes new laws
2. has senators and representatives
3. has two parts, or houses

Judicial
1. punishes people who break the law
2. explains the laws
3. makes sure that laws agree with the Constitution

Quiz

1. The form of government in the U.S. is called a democracy, or a democratic republic.
2. There are three branches of government: legislative, executive, and judicial.
3. The legislative branch makes the laws.
   The executive branch makes sure laws are obeyed.
   The judicial branch interprets the laws.

4. The two parts of Congress are the House of Representatives and the Senate.
5. There are 435 members in the House of Representatives.
6. The term of office for a representative is two years.
7. There are 100 members in the Senate.
8. The term of office for a senator is six years.
9. The term of office for a president is four years.
10. If the president cannot finish his term, the vice president takes his place.
11. A president can be elected twice.
12. The highest court in the land is the Supreme Court.
13. The president picks the judges on this court.
14. Judges on the Supreme Court can serve for life.
15. The Supreme Court is located in Washington, D.C.

CHAPTER 19
THE BILL OF RIGHTS
After You Read
1. T   4. T
2. F   5. F
3. F

Think About the Bill of Rights
Correct answers will vary.
1. A new law added to the Constitution is called an amendment.
2. The Bill of Rights is the first 10 amendments to the Constitution. The Bill of Rights helps to protect the liberty of people in the United States.
3. The Bill of Rights was adopted in 1791.
4. Some of the rights in the Bill of Rights are:
   the right to believe in any religion or no religion

the right to talk or write about anything a person wants
the right to a trial in court
the right to have a lawyer in court
the right to a fair, quick trial
5. Answers will vary.

Using New Words
1. trial   4. liberties
2. amendments   5. cruel
3. court

Sentence Completion
Correct answers will vary.
1. To change the Constitution, **we can add new amendments**.
2. The Bill of Rights is **the first 10 amendments to the Constitution**.
3. The Bill of Rights says that a person can talk **about anything he wants**.
4. The government cannot enter people's houses if it does not have **special permission**.

CHAPTER 20
OTHER AMENDMENTS
After You Read
1. T   4. T
2. F   5. F
3. T

Think About the Amendments to the Constitution
Correct answers will vary.
1. Two-thirds of each house of Congress must approve the amendment, and three-fourths of the states must approve it also.
2. Amendment 13 ended slavery.
3. Amendments 19, 24, and 26 make it easier for people to vote.
4. Amendment 16 gave the government the right to make more money by taxing the money people earn.
5. Answers will vary.

Using New Words
1. amendment   4. taxes
2. rights   5. function
3. slavery

Sentence Completion

Correct answers will vary.

1. Amendment 19 says that **women can vote**.
2. The newest amendment is **the twenty-sixth amendment**.
3. Amendment 26 says that **18-year-old citizens can vote**.
4. Answers will vary.

CHAPTER 21
THE VOTING PROCESS
After You Read

1. F   4. T
2. F   5. F
3. T

Think About Voting and Elections

Correct answers will vary.

1. The major political parties in the United States are the Democratic Party and the Republican Party.
2. Citizens of the United States can vote. The person must be at least 18 years old on the day of the election.
3. These amendments give voting rights to more people.
4. The three basic kinds of elections are national, state, and local.
5. A possible reason is that people must be able to prove their age and address.

Using New Words

1. registered   4. national
2. parties   5. Citizens
3. candidates

Sentence Completion

Correct answers will vary.

1. In national elections, people vote for **the president and the vice president**.
2. In state elections, people vote **for governors, senators, and other officials**.
3. In local elections, people **vote for leaders such as mayors**.
4. If a person wants to vote, **he or she must be at least 18 years old, be a citizen, and be a registered voter**.

CHAPTER REVIEW 4
Word Find

Match-up

1. c   5. e
2. d   6. f
3. g   7. b
4. h   8. a

Quiz

1. Yes, the Constitution can be changed by an amendment.
2. The Constitution has 26 amendments.
3. The Bill of Rights is the first 10 amendments to the Constitution.
4. Some of the rights guaranteed by the Bill of Rights are freedom of speech, freedom of religion, freedom of the press, and the right to a fair trial.
5. Some other important amendments are:
   13th: no more slavery
   19th: women can vote
   22nd: a person can only be elected president twice
   26th: lowered minimum voting age to 18
6. To vote you must be at least 18, a citizen of the U.S., live in your state a certain period of time, and be registered to vote.
7. The two major political parties are the Republican Party and the Democratic Party.

U.S. Department of Justice
Immigration and Naturalization Service

Application to Adjust Status from Temporary to Permanent Resident
(Under Section 245 A of Public Law 99-603)

Please read instructions: fee will not be refunded. INS Use: Bar Code SAMPLE **Address Label** (Place adhesive address label here from booklet **or** fill in name and address, and A 90 million file number in appropriate blocks.)	Fee Stamp Applicant's File No. A - 9 _ _ _ _ _ _ _ _

1. Family Name *(Last Name in CAPITAL Letters) (See instructions) (First Name) (Middle Name)*

2. Sex ☐ Male ☐ Female

3. Name as it appears on Temporary Resident Card *(I-688)* if different from above.

4. Phone No.'s *(Include Area Codes)*
Home:
Work:

5. Reason for difference in name *(See instructions)*

6. Home Address *(No. and Street)* *(Apt. No.)* *(City)* *(State)* *(Zip Code)*

7. Mailing Address *(if different)* *(Apt. No.)* *(City)* *(State)* *(Zip Code)*

8. **Place of Birth** *(City or Town)* *(County, Province or State)* *(Country)*

9. Date of Birth *(Month/Day/Year)*

10. **Your Mother's First Name**

11. **Your Father's First Name**

12. Enter your Social Security Number
_ _ _ - _ _ - _ _ _ _

13. Absences from the United States since becoming a Temporary Resident Alien. *(List most recent first.) (If you have a single absence in excess of 30 days or the total of all your absences exceeds 90 days, explain and attach any relevant information).*

Country	Purpose of Trip	From *(Month/Day/Year)*	To *(Month/Day/Year)*	Total Days Absent

14. When applying for temporary resident alien status, I
☐ did ☐ did not submit a medical examination form (I-693) with my application that included a serologic (blood) test for human immunodeficiency virus (HIV) infection. *(If you did not, submit a medical examination form (I-693) with this application that includes a serologic test for HIV.)*

15. Since becoming a temporary resident alien, I
☐ have ☐ have not been arrested, convicted or confined in a prison. *(If you have, provide the date(s), place(s), specific charge(s) and attach any relevant information.)*

16. Since becoming a temporary resident alien, I
☐ have ☐ have not been the beneficiary of a pardon, amnesty (other than legalization), rehabilitation decree, other act of clemency or similar action. *(If you have, explain and attach any relevant documentation.)*

17. Since becoming a temporary resident alien, I
☐ have ☐ have not received public assistance from any source, including but not limited to, the United States Government, any state, county, city or municipality. *(If you have, explain, including the name(s) and Social Security Number(s) used and attach any relevant information.)*

Form I-698 (08/10/88) Page 1

18. Concerning the requirement of minimal understanding of ordinary English and a knowledge and understanding of the history and government of the United States: *(Check appropriate block under Section A or B.)*

A. I will satisfy these requirements by;
  ☐ Examination at the time of interview for permanent residence.
  ☐ Satisfactorily pursuing a course of study recognized by the Attorney General.

B. I have satisfied these requirements by;
  ☐ Having satisfactorily pursued a course of study recognized by the Attorney General *(please attach appropriate documentation).*
  ☐ Exemption, in that I am 65 years of age or older, under the age of 16, or I am physically unable to comply. *(If physically unable to comply, explain and attach relevant documentation.)*

19. Applicants for status as Permanent Residents must establish that they are not excludable from the United States under the following provisions of section 212 of the INA. An applicant who is excludable under a provision of section 212 (a) which may not be waived is ineligible for permanent resident status. An applicant who is excludable under a provision of section 212 (a) which may be waived may, if otherwise eligible, be granted permanent resident status, if an application for waiver on form I-690 is filed and approved.

A. Grounds for exclusion which *may not be waived:*
  • Listed by paragraph number of section 212 (a):
  ____ (9) Aliens who have committed or who have been convicted of a crime involving moral turpitude (does not include minor traffic violations).
  ____ (10) Aliens who have been convicted of two or more offenses for which the aggregate sentences to confinement actually imposed were five years or more.
  ____ (15) Aliens likely to become a public charge.
  ____ (23) Aliens who have been convicted of a violation of any law or regulation relating to narcotic drugs or marihuana, or who have been illicit traffickers in narcotic drugs or marihuana.
  ____ (27) Aliens who intend to engage in activities prejudicial to the national interests or unlawful activities of a subversive nature.
  ____ (28) Aliens who are or at any time have been anarchists, or members of or affiliated with any Communist or other totalitarian party, including any subdivision or affiliate thereof.
  ____ (29) Aliens who have advocated or taught, either by personal utterance, or by means of any written matter, or through affiliation with an organization:
    1) Opposition to organized government;
    2) The overthrow of government by force or violence;
    3) The assaulting or killing of government officials because of their official character;
    4) The unlawful destruction of property;
    5) Sabotage, or;
    6) The doctrines of world communism, or the establishment of a totalitarian dictatorship in the United States.
  ____ (33) Aliens who, during the period beginning on March 23, 1933, and ending on May 8, 1945, under the direction of, and in association with:
    1) The Nazi government in Germany;
    2) Any government in any area occupied by the military forces of the Nazi government in Germany;
    3) Any government established with the assistance or cooperation of the Nazi government of Germany;
    4) Any government which was an ally of the Nazi government of Germany;
    ordered, incited, assisted or otherwise participated in the persecution of any person because of race, religion, national origin, or political opinion.
  • Provisions of 212 (e):
  ____ Aliens who at any time were exchange visitors subject to the two-year foreign residence requirement unless the requirement has been satisfied or waived pursuant to the provisions of section 212 (e) of the Act. (Does not apply to the Extended Voluntary Departure (EVD) class of temporary resident aliens).

Do any of the above classes apply to you?
☐ No ☐ Yes *(If "Yes", attach an explanation, and any relevant documentation. Place mark (X) on line before ground(s) of exclusion.)*

B. Grounds for exclusion which *may be waived:*
  • Listed by paragraph number of section 212 (a);
  ____ (1) Aliens who are mentally retarded.
  ____ (2) Aliens who are insane.
  ____ (3) Aliens who have suffered one or more attacks of insanity.
  ____ (4) Aliens afflicted with psychopathic personality, sexual deviation, or a mental defect.
  ____ (5) Aliens who are narcotic drug addicts or chronic alcoholics.
  ____ (6) Aliens who are afflicted with any dangerous contagious disease.
  ____ (7) Aliens who have a physical defect, disease or disability affecting their ability to earn a living.
  ____ (8) Aliens who are paupers, professional beggars or vagrants.
  ____ (11) Aliens who are polygamists or advocate polygamy.
  ____ (12) Aliens who are prostitutes or former prostitutes, or who have procured or attempted to procure or to import, prostitutes or persons for the purpose of prostitution or for any other immoral purpose, or aliens coming to the United States to engage in any other unlawful commercialized vice, whether or not related to prostitution.
  ____ (13) Aliens coming to the United States to engage in any immoral sexual act.
  ____ (16) Aliens who have been excluded from admission and deported and who again seek admission within one year from the date of such deportation.
  ____ (17) Aliens who have been arrested and deported and who reentered the United States within five years from the date of deportation.
  ____ (19) Aliens who have procured or have attempted to procure a visa or other documentation by fraud, or by willfully misrepresenting a material fact.
  ____ (22) Aliens who have applied for exemption or discharge from training or service in the Armed Forces of the United States on the ground of alienage and who have been relieved or discharged from such training or service.
  ____ (31) Aliens who at any time shall have, knowingly and for gain, encouraged, induced, assisted, abetted, or aided any other alien to enter or to try to enter the United States in violation of law.

Do any of the above classes apply to you?
☐ No ☐ Yes *(If "Yes", attach an explanation, and any relevant documentation and submit Form I-690. Place mark (X) on line before ground(s) of exclusion.)*

20. If your native alphabet is other than Roman letters, write your name in your native alphabet.	21. Language of native alphabet
22. Signature of Applicant - *I CERTIFY*, under penalty of perjury under the laws of the United States of America that the foregoing is true and correct. I hereby consent and authorize the Service to verify the information provided, and to conduct record checks pertinent to this application.	23. Date *(Month/Day/Year)*
24. Signature of person preparing form, if other than applicant. I DECLARE that this document was prepared by me at the request of the applicant and is based on all information of which I have any knowledge.	25. Date *(Month/Day/Year)*
26. Name and Address of person preparing form, **if other than applicant** *(type or print).*	27. Occupation

Page 2

121